CONTEMPORARY

P9-CTP-778

READING AND WRITING HANDBOOKS

WRITER'S MANUAL

EDWARD FRY, PH.D.
ELIZABETH SAKIEY, ED.D.

CONTEMPORARY BOOKS

a division of NTC/CONTEMPORARY PUBLISHING GROUP
Lincolnwood, Illinois USA

Library of Congress Cataloging-in-Publication Data
Fry, Edward Bernard, 1925–
    Writer's Manual / Edward Fry and Elizabeth Sakiey
            p. cm. —— (Contemporary's reading and writing handbooks)
        ISBN 0-8092-0878-4
        1. English language—Rhetoric—Handbooks, manuals, etc.
    2. English language—Grammar—Handbooks, manuals, etc. I. Title.
    II. Series.
    PE1408.F75 1996
    808'.042—dc20   96-44848
                                                                    CIP

ISBN: 0-8092-0878-4

Published by Contemporary Books,
a division of NTC/Contemporary Publishing Group, Inc.,
4255 West Touhy Avenue,
Lincolnwood (Chicago), Illinois, 60646-1975 U.S.A.

90 VG 9 8 7 6 5 4 3

Market Development Manager
Noreen Lopez

Editorial Development Director
Cynthia Krejcsi

Project Editor
Christine Kelner

Editorial
Sandra Hazel
Lisa Black

Production
Thomas D. Scharf

Cover and Interior Design
Kristy Sheldon

Production Artist
Denise M. Duffy

CONTENTS _____

INTRODUCTION

This manual was written as a handy resource for student writers. Designed for use either inside the classroom or for independent study, the *Writer's Manual* provides a quick reference to common spellings and basic rules for grammar and usage. It also presents the process of writing and a variety of techniques that help build strong writing skills, which will be helpful in other classes and settings where effective communication is necessary.

MECHANICS OF WRITING

Spelling Checker

The first and major portion of this book is an alphabetical list of nearly 7,000 common words used in writing. For checking spellings, it is much faster to use this list than to consult a dictionary because each Spelling Checker page contains many words. In addition, common variants (such as irregular plurals, participles, and adjective forms) are listed under their root word. For example, do you spell the participle of *run* as *runing* or *running?* The Spelling Rules on pages 67 and 68 will give you some guidance, but it may be faster and easier for new writers to simply look up the correct spelling in the word list.

Another useful feature of the Spelling Checker is that it groups words alphabetically under two-letter subheads. If you know only the first two letters of a word, you will find a relatively short list of words under that subhead. For example, under *ru* will be *rub, rude, rule, ruler,* and others. What's more, the list includes many of the most common compound words. Keep in mind that if you cannot find the word you seek as a compound, you should look for it as two separate words.

Homophones and frequently confused words are also listed in the Spelling Checker word list. For example, *write* and *right* are listed with brief definitions for both entries, as are *immigrate* and *emigrate.*

The Spelling Checker words have been selected from a scientifically determined list of 3,000 words (a frequency count) and their common variants, plus author-selected common words from the *Random House School Dictionary.* The list certainly doesn't contain all of the words needed by student writers, but it represents more than 95 percent of the words used by all writers. Additional words needed for effective writing are proper nouns, like *Chicago*; words specific to a subject, like *biopsy*; and advanced vocabulary words, like *sardonic.*

Word Endings and Suffixes

Many of the words in the Spelling Checker accept regular endings and suffixes; you simply add the endings and suffixes to the root word without changing the spelling of the root or the suffix. Here are the most common regular endings and suffixes:

-s	-er	-ful
-ed	-est	-less
-ing	-ly	-ness

Most of the words that require a change in spelling of the root or the ending/suffix are spelled out in the Spelling Checker list. These exceptions include words that call for doubling the final consonant before adding the ending, as in *running*, or using *-es* instead of just *-s* to form certain plurals. See Spelling Rules for more information.

There are a number of other less common endings that can be added to many of the root words. We don't intend to include every possible variant (inflected) form, just the most common. These suffixes are often just added to the root word, but for exceptions or different spellings, see the spelling rules beginning on page 67. Here are some of the less common suffixes:

-ion	-ate	-ability	-ial	-ary
-ive	-al	-ince	-ment	-ance
-ous	-able	-entail	-ory	

As a reminder, the following footnote appears at the bottom of every even-numbered page in the Spelling Checker:

> *The following regular endings/suffixes are not in the word list but can be added to the root word without changes:* -s, -ed, -ing, -er, -est, -ly, -ful, -less, *and* -ness. *Most exceptions and root changes are in the list.*

As a general rule, first look up the root word in the Spelling Checker. If you need a variant form using a regular ending, you should just add it to the root. If the root or ending requires a different spelling, it will be listed under the root word.

Prefixes

Prefixes are much less complicated than word endings and suffixes. In nearly every case the prefix is just added to the root word without any change in spelling. Here are a few of the most common prefixes:

un-	re-	in- (im-)	sub-
dis-	en- (em-)	non-	pre-
into-	over-	mis-	inter-

If you want to locate words using any of these prefixes, just look up the spelling of the root word in the Spelling Checker list and add the prefix needed. Don't change the root—that is why *misspell* has two *s*'s.

Spelling Rules, Spelling Using Phonics

Traditional spelling rules are not a lot of help for most writers. Mostly, these rules are concerned with the addition of endings or suffixes. For example, if the word ends in *x*, its plural is formed by adding *-es*, not just an *-s*. This rule and a few others are listed following the Spelling Checker (see page 67).

Somewhat more helpful are spelling rules related to phonics because when most writers try to spell an unknown word, they usually use some type of phonics. The Spelling Using Phonics charts (pages 70–73) will make this phonetic spelling more accurate. But as you probably already know, a lot of words that seem to be spelled correctly according to phonics rules are not correct according to the dictionary.

Capitalization, Punctuation

You can refer to these sections for basic rules and tips on selected topics.

Grammar

This manual does not attempt to be a complete grammar book, but it does contain many grammar basics; most important are the sections on sentences, verbs, and parts of speech.

METHODS OF WRITING

Guidelines for Composition

This section describes several types of writing and provides guidelines for letter writing, keeping a journal, creating stories, and producing other kinds of writing. An important article in this section discusses the writing process itself, something that experienced writers follow almost intuitively. If you have not done much writing, follow these steps and they will help you.

The last stage in improving your writing is proofreading to correct your errors. Whether you are correcting someone else's errors or someone is correcting your writing, it is convenient to use standard proofreading symbols. A page of the most common symbols is included for you.

Techniques for Composition

This section offers several boosts to your creativity. First, Ways of Organizing Your Thoughts suggests general methods for developing your topic and for putting your material into an effective order. Then, Story Starters, Tips on Improving Your Vocabulary, and Literary Terms and Devices provide help for specific problems or weaknesses. Story starters are interesting opening phrases for a story, just to get you started. An example would be "If I won a million dollars. . . ." The story starter concept has been expanded in this book to include suggestions for titles, ways to end a story, and thought-provoking questions, all of which should produce some interesting story writing ideas.

Not everyone is aware of literary devices, that is, techniques that writers use. When a writer uses them well, however, his or her writing is stronger and more appealing. The list of terms and techniques in this book will help you become more conscious of ways to add sparkle to your writing.

You can study the terms one at a time and then learn more about them by trying to use them in a trial paragraph or story that you are writing. Or, you can just pick out one or two and insert them into an already existing story to see how it might be improved.

ADDITIONAL HELP
Personal Spelling List
Finally, there is the Personal Spelling List. This useful section encourages you to keep a list of words that you have had to look up. Maintaining this list serves two purposes: (1) it helps you to learn the correct spelling of the word, and (2) it provides a handy reference for quickly looking up words that you may need.

Don't be embarrassed to write even common words in your personal spelling list. Everybody has certain words that present continual difficulty.

In Conclusion
Take just a few minutes to look at each of the sections in the second half of the book. Doing so will give you a review and an overview of grammar, usage, and writing skills, making this book a really useful tool for you.

NOTE: Irregular plurals, participles, and adjective forms are listed under the root word.

a

a

ab

ability
  abilities
able
  abler
  ablest
  ably
aboard
about
above
absent
absorb

ac

accent
accept *(to receive)*
  [except *(to exclude)*]
accident
  accidental
accommodate
  accommodated
  accommodating
accompany
  accompanied
  accompanies
  accompaniment
account
  accountant
accurate
  accuracy
ache
  ached
  aching
achieve
  achieved
  achiever
  achieving
  achievement
acid
acorn
acre
acrobat
  acrobatic
across
act
  action
  active
  activities

activity
actor
actress
actual

ad

ad *(advertisement)*
  [add *(find the sum)*]
adapt
add *(find the sum)*
  [ad *(advertisement)*]
  adds *(combines)*
  [ads *(advertisements)*]
  [adz *(axlike tool)*]
addend
  addenda
addict
addition
  additional
address
adjective
adjust
administer
  administration
  administrator
admire
admit
  admission
  admitted
  admitting
adopt
  adoption
ads *(advertisements)*
  [adds *(combines)*]
  [adz *(axlike tool)*]
adult
advance
  advanced
  advancer
  advancing
advantage
adventure
  adventured
  adventurer
  adventuresome
  adventuring
  adventurous
adverb
advice
adz *(axlike tool)*
  [adds *(combines)*]
  [ads *(advertisements)*]

af

affair
affect *(act on)*
  [effect *(something produced)*]
  affection
afford
afraid
Africa
  African
after
afternoon
afterward

ag

again
against
age
  aged
  aging
agent
ago
aggravate *(made worse)*
  [agitate *(stir up)*]
agree
  agreed
  agreement
agriculture
  agricultural
  agriculturally

ah

ah
ahead

ai

aid *(help)*
  [aide *(assistant)*]
ail *(be sick)*
  [ale *(beverage)*]
aim
air *(what you breathe)*
  [heir *(successor)*]
airline
airmail
airplane
airport
aisle *(narrow path)*
  [I'll *(I will)*]
  [isle *(island)*]

al

Alabama
alarm
Alaska
  Alaskan
alcohol
  alcoholic
ale *(beverage)*
  [ail *(be sick)*]
alike
alive
all *(everything)*
  [awl *(pointed tool)*]
alley
alligator
allow
  [allowed *(permitted)*]
  [aloud *(audible)*]
ally
  allied
  allies
  allying
almost
alone
along
aloud *(audible)*
  [allowed *(permitted)*]
alphabet
  alphabetic
  alphabetical
already *(previously)*
  [all ready *(completely prepared or ready)*]
also
altar *(raised church table)*
  [alter *(change)*]
although
altitude
altogether *(completely)*
  [all together *(in a group)*]
aluminum
always

am

am *(irreg. vb)*
amaze
  amazed
  amazing

America
  American
among
amount
amuse
  amused
  amusing

an

an
ancestor
anchor
anchorwoman
ancient
and
angel
anger
angle
  angled
  angler
  angling
angry
  angrier
  angrily
animal
announce
  announced
  announcer
  announcing
annoy
annual
another
answer
ant *(insect)*
  [aunt *(parent's sister)*]
anxious
any
anybody
anyone
anything
anyway *(adverb)*
  [any way *(adjective and noun)*]
anywhere

ap

apart
apartment
apology

apostrophe
apparent
appeal
appear
  appearance
apple
applesauce
apply
  applied
  applier
  applies
appoint
  appointee
approach
  approaches
appropriate
approve
approximate
  approximated
April
apron

ar

Arab
  Arabian
  Arabic
arc *(arched curve)*
  [ark *(a boat)*]
arch
Arctic
are *(irreg. vb)*
area
aren't *(are not)*
Argentina
argue
  argument
  argumentative
arithmetic
Arizona
ark *(a boat)*
  [arc *(arched curve)*]
Arkansas
arm

The following regular endings/suffixes are not in the word list but can be added to the root word without changes: -s, -ed, -ing, -er, -est, -ly, -ful, -less, and -ness. Most exceptions and root changes are in the list.

army
    armies
around
arrange
    arranged
    arrangement
    arranger
    arranging
arrive
    arrival
    arrived
    arriving
arrow
art
article
artist
    artistic
    artistically

as

as
ascend
    ascension
    ascent *(a climb)*
    [assent *(agree)*]
ash
    ashes
    ashtray
Asia
    Asian
aside
ask
asleep
assemble
    assembly
    assemblies
assent *(agree)*
    [ascent *(a climb)*]
assistance *(help)*
    [assistants *(those who help)*]
associate
    associated
    associating
    association
assume
    assumed
    assuming

astronaut
astronomer
astronomical
astronomy

at

at
ate *(did eat)*
    [eight *(the number 8)*]
Atlantic
atmosphere
    atmospheric
atom
    atomic
attach
    attaches
attack
attempt
attend
    attendance *(being present)*
    [attendants *(escorts)*]
attention
attitude
attract
    attractive

au

audience
August
aunt *(parent's sister)*
    [ant *(insect)*]
aural *(of the ears)*
    [oral *(by way of mouth)*]
Australia
    Australian
Austria
    Austrian
autoharp
author
authority
    authorities
automatic
    automatically
automation
automobile
autonomy
    autonomous

autumn
    autumnal
auxiliary
    auxiliaries

av

avail
    availability
    available
average
    averaged
    averaging
avocation
avoid
    avoidable

aw

awake *(irreg. vb)*
    awaking
aware
    awareness
away *(gone)*
    [aweigh *(to clear anchor)*]
awesome
awful *(terrible)*
    [offal *(entrails)*]
    awfully
awl *(pointed tool)*
    [all *(everything)*]

ax

ax
    axes
axis
axle

ay

aye *(yes)*
    [eye *(organ of sight)*]
    [I *(myself)*]

ba

baby
  babied
  babies
back
background
backward
backyard
bacon
bacteria
  bacterial
bad
bag
  bagged
  bagger
  bagging
bail *(scoop out water)*
  [bale *(bundle)*]
bait *(lure)*
  [bate *(lessen)*]
bake
  baked
  baker
  baking
bakery
  bakeries
balance
  balanced
  balancer
  balancing
bale *(bundle)*
  [bail *(scoop out water)*]
ball *(round object)*
  [bawl *(to cry)*]
ballet
ballgame
balloon
Baltimore
banana
band *(united group)*
  [banned *(forbidden)*]
bandage
  bandaged
  bandaging
bang
bank

banned *(forbidden)*
  [band *(united group)*]
bar
  barred *(shut out)*
  [bard *(a poet)*]
  barring
bard *(a poet)*
  [barred *(shut out)*]
bare *(nude)*
  [bear *(an animal)*]
  bared
  baring *(uncovering)*
  [bearing *(manner of acting)*]
bareback
barefoot
bark
barn
barrel
base *(bottom of a structure)*
  [bass *(lowest voice)*]
  based
  bases *(more than one base)*
  [basis *(foundation)*]
  basing
baseball
basic
basin
basis *(foundation)*
  bases *(more than one base)*
basket
basketball
bass *(lowest voice)*
  [base *(bottom of a structure)*]
bat
  batted
  batter
  batting
bate *(lessen)*
  [bait *(lure)*]
bath
bathroom
batter

battery
  batteries
battle
  battled
  battler
  battling
bawl *(to cry)*
  [ball *(round object)*]
bay

be

be *(exist) (irreg. vb)*
  [bee *(an insect)*]
  being
beach *(shore)*
  [beech *(type of tree)*]
  beaches
bead
beam
bean
bear *(an animal)*
  [bare *(nude)*]
  bearing *(manner of acting)*
  [baring *(uncovering)*]
beast
beat *(whip) (irreg. vb)*
  [beet *(type of vegetable)*]
  beating
beau *(boyfriend)*
  [bow *(decorative knot)*]
beauty
  beauties
  beautiful
beaver
became
because
become
  becoming
bed
  bedded
  bedding
bedroom
bedspread

The following regular endings/suffixes are not in the word list but can be added to the root word without changes: -s, -ed, -ing, -er, -est, -ly, -ful, -less, and -ness. Most exceptions and root changes are in the list.

bee *(an insect)*
　[be *(exist)*]
beech *(type of tree)*
　[beach *(shore)*]
beef
been *(used to be)*
　[bin *(a box)*]
beep
beer *(a drink)*
　[bier *(a coffin)*]
beet *(type of vegetable)*
　[beat *(whip)*]
beetle
before
beg
　beggar
　begged
　begging
began
begin *(irreg. vb)*
　beginning
begun
behalf
behave
　behaved
　behaving
behavior
　behavioral
behind
being
Belgium
belief
believable
believe
　believed
　believer
　believing
bell *(something you ring)*
　[belle *(pretty girl)*]
belly
belong
below
belt
bench
　benches
bend *(irreg. vb)*
beneath
benefit
bent
berry *(type of fruit)*
　[bury *(put in ground)*]
　berries

berth *(place to sleep)*
　[birth *(being born)*]
beside
best
bet *(irreg. vb)*
　betting
　bettor
　[better *(more good)*]
betray
better *(more good)*
　[bettor *(one who bets)*]
between
beyond

bi

Bible
bicycle
　bicycled
　bicycling
bid
bier *(coffin)*
　[beer *(a drink)*]
big
　bigger
　biggest
　bigness
bike
bill
　billed *(did bill)*
　[build *(construct)*]
billfold
billion
bin *(a box)*
　[been *(used to be)*]
biology
bird
birth *(being born)*
　[berth *(a place to sleep)*]
birthday
bit
bite *(irreg. vb)*
　biting
bitter
bizarre

bl

blab
black
　blacken
　blackish
blackbird

blackboard
blackout
blade
blame
　blamed
　blaming
blank
blanket
blast
blaze
　blazed
　blazing
bled
bleed *(irreg. vb)*
blend
blew *(did blow)*
　[blue *(a color)*]
blind
blink
block
blood
　bloodied
　bloodier
　bloodies
　bloodiest
　bloody
bloodhound
bloom
blossom
blouse
blow
　blew *(did blow)*
　[blue *(a color)*]
blue *(a color)*
　[blew *(did blow)*]
blueprint
bluff

bo

boar *(pig)*
　[bore *(uninteresting)*]
board *(1. plank, 2. get on, 3. lodge)*
　[bored *(uninterested)*]
　boarder *(one who boards)*
　[border *(boundary)*]
boat
body
　bodies

boil
bold
   bolder *(more bold)*
   [boulder *(large rock)*]
Bolivia
boll *(cotton pod)*
   [bowl *(1. a dish,
   2. play tenpins)*]
bond
bone
   boned
   boning
bonnet
bonus
boo
book
bookkeeper
boom
boost
boot
border *(boundary)*
   [boarder *(one who
   boards)*]
bore *(uninteresting)*
   [boar *(pig)*]
   bored *(uninterested)*
   [board *(1. plank,
   2. get on, 3. lodge)*]
born *(brought into life)*
   [borne *(carried)*]
borough *(part of a city)*
   [burro *(donkey)*]
   [burrow *(to dig)*]
borrow
boss
   bossy
Boston
   Bostonian
both
bother
bottle
   bottled
   bottler
   bottling
bottom
bough *(limb of a tree)*
   [bow *(front end of a ship)*]
bought

bouillon *(clear broth)*
   [bullion *(uncoined
   gold or silver)*]
boulder *(large rock)*
   [bolder *(more bold)*]
bounce
bound
boundary
   boundaries
bow *(decorating knot)*
   [beau *(boyfriend)*]
   bow *(front end of a ship)*
   [bough *(limb of a tree)*]
bowl *(1. dish, 2. play tenpins)*
   [boll *(cotton pod)*]
box
   boxes
boy *(male child)*
   [buoy *(floating marker)*]

br

bracelet
brag
brain
   brainy
brake *(device for
   stopping vehicles)*
   [break *(take apart by force)*]
   braked
   braking
branch
   branches
brand
brass
   brasses
   brassy
brave
   braved
   braver
   bravest
   braving
Brazil
   Brazilian
bread *(food)*
   [bred *(raised)*]
break *(take apart by
   force) (irreg. vb)*
   [brake *(device for
   stopping vehicles)*]

breakfast
breath
breathe
   breathable
   breathed
   breather
   breathing
bred *(raised)*
   [bread *(food)*]
breeze
   breezed
   breezing
brew
   brewed *(made beer, tea, etc.)*
   [brood *(group of
   offspring)*]
   brews
   [bruise *(an injury)*]
brick
bridal *(relating to a bride)*
   [bridle *(part of a horse
   harness)*]
bridge
   bridged
   bridging
bridle *(part of a horse harness)*
   [bridal *(relating to a bride)*]
brief
bright
brilliant
bring *(irreg. vb)*
Britain
   British
broad
broadcast
broke
   broken
brood *(group of
   offspring)*
   [brewed *(made beer, tea, etc.)*]
brook
brother
brought
brown
bruise *(an injury)*
   [brews *(makes beer, tea, etc.)*]
brush
   brushes

The following regular endings/suffixes are not in the word list but can be added to the root word without changes: -s, -ed, -ing, -er, -est, -ly, -ful, -less, and -ness. Most exceptions and root changes are in the list.

bu

bubble
  bubbled
  bubbling
  bubbly
buck
bucket
bud
  budded
  budding
buffalo
  buffaloes
bug
build *(construct) (irreg. vb)*
  [billed *(did bill)*]
built
bulb
Bulgaria
bull
bulldog
bullet
bullion *(uncoined gold or silver)*
  [bouillon *(clear broth)*]
bump
bunch
  bunches
bundle
  bundled
  bundling
buoy *(floating marker)*
  [boy *(male child)*]
burn
burro *(donkey)*
  [borough *(part of a city)*]
  [burrow *(to dig)*]
burst *(irreg. vb)*
bury *(put in ground)*
  [berry *(type of fruit)*]
bus
  buses
bush
  bushes
bushy
  bushier
  bushiest
  bushiness

business
  businesses
bust
busy
  busied
  busier
  busiest
  busily
but *(except)*
  [butt *(the hindmost end)*]
butter
buttercup
buttery
butterfly
  butterflies
buttermilk
button
buy *(purchase) (irreg. vb)*
  [by *(beside)*]
  [bye *(farewell)*]

by

by *(beside)*
  [buy *(purchase)*]
  [bye *(farewell)*]

ca

cabbage
cabin
cabinet
cache *(hiding place for goods)*
  [cash *(money)*]
cage
  caged
  caging
cake
  caked
  caking
calf
  calves
California
  Californian
call
callous *(unfeeling)*
  [callus *(hardened skin tissue)*]
calm

came
camel
camera
camp
campaign
campfire
can
  canned
  canner
  canning
Canada
  Canadian
canal
candle
candy
  candied
  candies
cane
cannon *(large military gun)*
  [canon *(law)*]
can't *(cannot)*
canvas *(sturdy cloth)*
  [canvass *(survey)*]
canyon
cap
  capped
  capping
capable
capacity
cape
capital *(1. money, 2. seat of government)*
  [capitol *(a statehouse)*]
captain
capture
  captured
  capturing
car
carat *(jeweler's measure)*
  [caret *(proofreader's mark)*]
  [carrot *(a vegetable)*]
carbon
  carbonation
card
cardboard
care
  caring
career

caret *(proofreader's mark)*
  [carat *(jeweler's measure)*]
  [carrot *(a vegetable)*]
cargo
  cargoes
carol *(a song)*
  [carrel *(study space in
  a library)*]
carpet
carpool
carrel *(study space in a library)*
  [carol *(a song)*]
carriage
carrot *(a vegetable)*
  [carat *(jeweler's measure)*]
  [caret *(proofreader's mark)*]
carry
  carried
  carrier
  carries
cart
carve
  carved
  carver
  carving
case
  cased
  casing
cash *(money)*
  [cache *(hiding place
  for goods)*]
  cashier
cast *(actors in a play)*
  [caste *(social class)*]
castle
casual
cat
catch *(irreg. vb)*
  catches
caterpillar
cattail
cattle
Caucasian
caught
cause
  caused
  causing

caution
cave
  caved
  caving

ce

cede *(give over; surrender)*
  [seed *(part of a plant)*]
ceiling *(top of a room)*
  [sealing *(closing)*]
celebrant
celebrate
  celebrated
  celebrating
  celebration
  celebrator
cell *(prison room)*
  [sell *(exchange for money)*]
cellar *(basement)*
  [seller *(one who sells)*]
cement
censor *(to ban)*
  [sensor *(detection device)*]
cent *(penny)*
  [sent *(did send)*]
  [scent *(odor)*]
center
central
cents *(money)*
  [sense *(feel)*]
century
  centuries
cereal *(food made from grain)*
  [serial *(of a series)*]
ceremony
certain
  certainty
cession *(yielding)*
  [session *(a meeting)*]

ch

chain
chair
chalk
challenge
  challenged

challenger
challenging
chamber
champion
  championship
chance
  chanced
  chancing
change
  changeable
  changed
  changing
channel
chapter
character
  characteristic
  characteristically
charge
  charged
  charging
charm
chart
chase
  chased *(did chase)*
  [chaste *(pure)*]
  chaser
  chasing
chat
  chatter
  chatty
cheap *(inexpensive)*
  [cheep *(a bird sound)*]
cheat
check
cheek
cheep *(a bird sound)*
  [cheap *(inexpensive)*]
cheer
cheese
chemical
cherry
  cherries
chest
chic *(stylish)*
  [sheik *(Arab chief)*]
  chicly

The following regular endings/suffixes are not in the word list but can be added to the root word without changes: -s, -ed, -ing, -er, -est, -ly, -ful, -less, *and* -ness. *Most exceptions and root changes are in the list.*

Chicago
  Chicagoan
chicken
chief
child
  children
Chile *(South American country)*
  [chili *(hot pepper)*]
  [chilly *(cold)*]
  Chilean
chimney
chin
China
  Chinese
chip
chocolate
choice
choir *(singing group)*
  [quire *(paper quantity)*]
choke
  choker
  choking
choose *(irreg. vb)*
  choosing
  choosy
chop
choral *(of a choir)*
  [coral *(sea-animal skeleton)*]
chorale *(sacred hymn)*
  [corral *(pen for livestock)*]
chord *(group of musical notes)*
  [cord *(string)*]
chorus
  choruses
chose
  chosen
Christ
  Christian
chromosome
chronological
chubby
chuckle
church
  churches
chute *(slide)*
  [shoot *(discharge gun)*]

ci

circle
  circled
  circling
circuit
circus
  circuses
cite *(give credit to a source)*
  [sight *(vision)*]
  [site *(location)*]
citizen
city
  cities
civil
  civilian
  civilization
  civilize
  civilized
  civilizing

cl

claim
  claimant
clam
clap
  clapped
  clapper
  clapping
clash
clasp
class
  classes
classify
  classification
  classifier
  classifies
classmate
classroom
clause *(part of a sentence)*
  [claws *(hooked nails on animals' feet)*]
claw
  claws *(hooked nails on animals' feet)*
  [clause *(part of a sentence)*]
clay
clean
clear

clerk
Cleveland
clever
click *(short, sharp sound)*
  [clique *(group of friends)*]
cliff
climate
climax
climb *(to ascend)*
  [clime *(climate)*]
cling
clip
clipboard
clique *(group of friends)*
  [click *(short, sharp sound)*]
cloak
clock
  clocked
  clocking
close *(shut)*
  [clothes *(clothing)*]
  closed
  closes
  closing
close *(near)*
  closer
  closest
cloth
clothe
  clothed
  clothing
clothes *(clothing)*
  [close *(shut)*]
clothesline
clothespin
cloud
club
clue *(hint, helps solve a mystery)*
  [clew *(a ball of yarn)*]

co

coach
  coaches
coal *(fuel)*
  [cole *(cabbage)*]
coarse *(rough)*
  [course *(1. path, 2. school subject)*]

coast
    coastal
coat
coax
    coaxes
code
    coded
    coder
    coding
coffee
coil
coin
cold
cole *(cabbage)*
    [coal *(fuel)*]
collage
collapse
    collapsed
    collapsing
collar
collect
    collector
    collection
college
    collegiate
collide
    collision
Colombia
colonel *(military officer)*
    [kernel *(a seed or grain)*]
colony
    colonies
    colonial
    colonist
color
Colorado
Columbus
column
coma *(state of unconsciousness)*
    [comma *(punctuation)*]
comb
combat
combine
    combined
    combination
    combining

come *(irreg. vb)*
    coming
comedy
    comedies
comet
comfort
    comfortable
    comfortably
comic
    comical
comma *(punctuation)*
    [coma *(state of unconsciousness)*]
command
commence
    commenced
    commencing
commend
    commendable
    commendably
    commendation
comment
commerce
    commercial
    commercialism
commission
commit
    commitment
committee
common
commotion
communicate
    communicated
    communicating
    communication
    communicator
Communist
    Communism
community
    communities
compact
companion
company
    companies
compare
    compared
    comparing
    comparison

compass
    compasses
compatible
compel
compensate
    compensated
    compensating
compete
competent
competition
complain
complement *(completing part)*
    [compliment *(praise)*]
    complementary *(completes)*
    [complimentary *(free)*]
complete
    completed
    completing
complex
    complexes
complexion
complicate
    complicated
    complication
compliment *(praise)*
    [complement *(completing part)*]
    complimentary *(free)*
    [complementary *(completes)*]
component
compose
    composed
    composer
    composing
composite
    composition
compound
comprehend
    comprehension
compress
    compression
    compressor
compromise
compute
    computation
    computed
    computer
    computing

The following regular endings/suffixes are not in the word list but can be added to the root word without changes: -s, -ed, -ing, -er, -est, -ly, -ful, -less, and -ness. Most exceptions and root changes are in the list.

comrade
concave
conceal
conceive
    conceived
concentrate
    concentrated
    concentrating
    concentration
concept
    conceptual
    conception
concern
concert
concession
conclude
    conclusion
concrete
condemn
    condemnation
condense
    condensed
condition
conduct
    conductor
cone
conference
confess
    confession
confide
    confident
    confidential
confine
    confined
    confining
confirm
conflict
conform
confront
    confrontation
confuse
    confused
    confusing
    confusion
congress
    congresses
    congressional
congruent
conjunction
connect
    connection
    connector

Connecticut
connotation
conquer
    conqueror
conscience (*noun*)
    [conscious (*adjective*)]
consecutive
consent
consequence
conserve
    conservation
consider
    considerable
    considerably
    considerate
consist
    consistence
    consistency
    consistent
consonant
constant
constitution
    constitutional
construct
    construction
consult
    consultation
consume
    consumed
    consumer
    consuming
    consumption
contact
contagious (*easily spread*)
    [contiguous (*near or close*)]
contain
content
contest
    contestant
continent
    continental
continual (*no interruption,*
    again and again)
    [continuous (*uninterrupted,*
    unbroken)]
    continually
continue
    continued
    continuing

continuous (*uninterrupted,*
unbroken)
    [continual (*no interruption,*
    again and again)]
contract
contraction
contrary
contrast
contribute
    contributed
    contributing
    contribution
    contributor
control
    controllable
    controlled
    controller
    controlling
controversy
    controversial
convenient
    convenience
convention
    conventional
conversation
    conversational
converse
convert
    convertible
convex
convict
    conviction
convince
    convinced
    convincing
cook
cookie
cool
coop (*chicken pen*)
    [coupe (*type of car*)]
cop-out
copper
copperhead
copy
    copied
    copier
    copies
copyright
coral (*sea-animal skeleton*)
    [choral (*of a choir*)]

cord (string)
　　[chord (group of
　　musical notes)]
　　cordless
core (the center)
　　[corps (group of
　　military personnel)]
　　cored
　　coring
corn
corner
corps (group of
　　military personnel)
　　[core (the center)]
corral (pen for livestock)
　　[chorale (sacred
　　hymn)]
correct
　　correction
correspond
　　correspondence
　　correspondent
corrupt
cosmic
cost (irreg. vb)
Costa Rica
costume
　　costumed
　　costuming
cottage
cotton
couch
cough
could
couldn't (could not)
council (legislative body)
　　[counsel (to advise)]
counsel (to advise)
　　[council (legislative
　　body)]
　　counselor
count
country
　　countries
county
　　counties
coupe (type of car)
　　[coop (chicken pen)]

couple
　　coupled
　　coupling
courage
　　courageous
course (1. path,
　　2. school subject)
　　[coarse (rough)]
　　coursed
　　coursing
court
cousin
cover
cow
coward
cowboy

cr

crack
craft
　　crafty
crash
　　crashes
crawl
crayon
crazy
　　crazier
　　craziest
　　crazily
creak (squeaking sound)
　　[creek (a stream)]
cream
　　creamy
create
　　created
　　creating
　　creation
　　creative
　　creator
creature
credible
credit
　　creditor
credulous
creek (a stream)
　　[creak (squeaking
　　sound)]

creep (irreg. vb)
crept
crew
　　crews (groups of workers)
　　[cruise (an ocean voyage)]
crib
crocodile
crop
　　cropped
　　cropping
cross
crosswalk
crow
crowd
crown
cruel
cruise (an ocean voyage)
　　[crews (groups of workers)]
crush
　　crushes
crust
cry
　　cried
　　crier
　　cries
crystal

cu

cub
Cuba
cube
　　cubed
　　cubing
cue (to prompt)
　　[queue (line of people)]
culture
　　cultural
　　cultured
　　culturist
cup
　　cupped
　　cupping
cupboard
cupcake
curious
　　curiosity
curl

The following regular endings/suffixes are not in the word list but can be added to the root word without changes: -s, -ed, -ing, -er, -est, -ly, -ful, -less, and -ness. Most exceptions and root changes are in the list.

current *(1. recent,*
    2. fast-flowing part of a
    stream)
    [currant *(small*
    raisin)]
curser *(one who curses)*
    [cursor *(moving*
    pointer on
    computer screen)]
curtain
curvature
curve
    curved
    curving
cushion
custom
    customs
cut
    cutting
cutout

cy

cycle
    cycled
    cycling
    cyclist
cyclone
cylinder
    cylindrical
cymbal *(a percussion*
    instrument)
    [symbol *(a sign)*]

cz

Czech Republic

da

dad
daily
dairy
    dairies
Dallas
dam *(stop flow)*
    [damn *(curse)*]
    dammed
    damming
damage
    damaged
    damages
    damaging

damp
dance
    danced
    dancer
    dances
    dancing
danger
    dangerous
dare
    dared
    daring
dark
    darken
dash
date
    dated
    dating
datum
    data
daughter
dawn
day
    days *(parts of a week)*
    [daze *(to stun and confuse)*]
daydream
daylight
daytime
daze *(to stun and confuse)*
    [days *(parts of a week)*]

de

dead
deaf
deal
    dealt
dear *(much loved)*
    [deer *(type of animal)*]
death
decease
December
decide
    decided
    deciding
decimal
decision
deck
declare
    declaration
    declared
    declaring

deep
    deepen
deer *(type of animal)*
    [dear *(much loved)*]
defeat
defect
defense
    defensible
    defensive
define
    defined
    defining
definite
    definition
degree
Delaware
delay
delicate
delicious
delight
delinquent
    delinquency
    delinquencies
deliver
    deliverance
    deliveries
    delivery
demand
Denmark
    Danish
denominator
dense
    denser
    densities
    density
Denver
deny
    denial
    denied
depart
department
depend
    dependable
    dependence
    dependency
    dependent
deposit
    depositor
depth
deputy

derive
  derived
  deriving
describe
  described
  describing
  description
desert *(leave)*
  [dessert *(pie)*]
  desertion
design
designate
  designated
  designating
  designation
desire
  desirable
  desired
  desiring
desk
despite
despot
dessert *(pie)*
  [desert *(leave)*]
destroy
destruction
detail
determine
  determined
  determining
Detroit
develop
  development
  developmental
device
devil
deviltry
dew *(water)*
  [do *(perform)*]
  [due *(owe)*]

di

diagnosis
diagonal
diagram
  diagrammed
  diagramming

dial
diameter
diamond
dictionary
  dictionaries
did
didn't *(did not)*
die *(stop living)*
  [dye *(color)*]
  died
  dying
diet
  dietitian
differ
  difference
  different
  differentiate
difficult
  difficulties
  difficulty
dig *(irreg. vb)*
  digger
  digging
digit
  digital
dim
  dimmed
  dimmer
  dimmest
dime
dimension
  dimensional
dine
  dined
  diner
  dining
dinner
dinosaur
dip
direct
  direction
  director
dirt
  dirtier
  dirtiest
  dirty
disable

disagree
  disagreeable
  disagreement
disappear
  disappearance
disappoint
disapprove
disaster
disburse *(pay out)*
  [disperse *(scatter)*]
discomfort
discourage
discover
  discoveries
  discovery
discreet *(wisely cautious)*
  [discrete *(separate)*]
discrepancy
  discrepancies
discriminate
discuss
  discusses
  discussion
disease
disguise
dish
  dishes
dishpan
disinterested *(impartial or without prejudice)*
  [uninterested *(indifferent or without interest)*]
dislike
disperse *(scatter)*
  [disburse *(pay out)*]
display
dispute
disrupt
dissolve
  dissolved
  dissolving
distant
  distance
distinguish
  distinguishable
  distinguishes
dive *(irreg. vb)*
  diver
  diving

The following regular endings/suffixes are not in the word list but can be added to the root word without changes: -s, -ed, -ing, -er, -est, -ly, -ful, -less, and -ness. Most exceptions and root changes are in the list.

diverge
  diverged
  diverging
diverse
  diversify
divide
  divided
  dividing
  divisibility
  divisible
  division
divulge
  divulged
  divulging

do

do (perform) (irreg. vb)
  [dew (water droplets)]
  [due (payable)]
dock
doctor
doe (female deer)
  [dough (bread mixture)]
does
doesn't (does not)
dog
doll
dollar
done (finished)
  [dun (1. demand payment,
    2. dull color)]
donkey
don't (do not)
door
doorknob
doorway
dot
  dotted
  dotting
double
  doubled
  doubling
doubt
dough (bread mixture)
  [doe (female deer)]
dove
down
  downed
downpour
downstairs
downtown
downward
dozen

dr

drag
  dragged
  dragging
dragon
dragonfly
dramatic
  dramatically
drank
draw (irreg. vb)
drawbridge
drawer
dream (irreg. vb)
  dreamy
dress
  dresses
drew
drift
drill
  drilled
  driller
  drilling
drink (irreg. vb)
drive (irreg. vb)
  driver
  driving
drive-in
driveway
drop
  dropped
  dropping
dropout
drove
drown
drug
  drugged
drugstore
drum
  drummed
  drummer
  drumming
drunk
dry
  dried
  drier
  dries
  driest

du

dual (two)
  [duel (formal combat)]

duck
  ducked (did duck)
  [duct (tube or pipe)]
due (payable)
  [dew (water droplets)]
  [do (perform)]
duel (formal combat)
  [dual (two)]
dug
duke
dull
  dully
dump
dumb
dun (1. demand payment,
    2. dull color)
  [done (finished)]
during
dust
Dutch
duty
  duties

dy

dye (color)
  [die (stop living)]
  dyed

ea

each
eager
eagle
ear
early
  earlier
  earliest
earn (work for)
  [urn (vase)]
earth
earthquake
ease
  eased
  easing
easily
east
eastern
easy
  easier
  easiest
eat (irreg. vb)

eb

ebb
ebony

ec

echo
   echoes
economy
   economic
   economies
Ecuador

ed

edge
   edged
   edger
   edging
educate
   education

ee

eerie
   eerier
   eerily
   eeriness

ef

effect *(something produced)*
   [affect *(act on)*]
effective
efficient
   efficiency
effort

eg

egg
Egypt
   Egyptian

ei

eight *(the number 8)*
   [ate *(did eat)*]
eighth

eighteen
   eighteenth
eighty
   eighties
   eightieth
either

el

elect
   election
   elector
electric
   electrical
   electrician
   electricity
electron
   electronic
element
elephant
elevate
   elevated
   elevating
   elevation
elevator
eleven
   eleventh
else

em

emigrate *(leave your country)*
   [immigrate *(come to a country to live)*]
   emigrated
   emigrating
   emigration
eminent *(famous, outstanding)*
   [imminent *(threat to occur at any moment)*]
emotional
emperor
empire
employ
   employable
empty
   emptied
   emptier

   empties
   emptiness

en

enable
   enabled
   enabling
enclose
   enclosure
encourage
   encouraged
   encouraging
encyclopedia
end
enemy
   enemies
energy
   energies
enforce
engage
   engaged
   engaging
engine
engineer
England
   English
enjoy
   enjoyable
enormous
enough
ensure *(make certain)*
   [insure *(to issue or obtain insurance)*]
   ensured
   ensuring
enter
entertain
entire
entrance
entry
   entries
environment
   environmental

The following regular endings/suffixes are not in the word list but can be added to the root word without changes: -s, -ed, -ing, -er, -est, -ly, -ful, -less, and -ness. Most exceptions and root changes are in the list.

eq

equal
    equality
equation
equator
equip
    equipped
    equipping
equipment
equivalent

er

erase
    eraser
    erasing
error
    erroneous
erupt
    eruption

es

escape
    escaped
    escaping
Eskimo
especial
essential
establish
    establishes
estimate
    estimated
    estimating
    estimation
    estimator

eu

Europe
    European

ev

even
evening
event
eventual
ever
every
everybody
everyday *(routine, common)*
    [every day *(each day)*]

everyone
everything
everywhere
evidence
    evidenced
evil

ew

ewe *(female sheep)*
    [yew *(a shrub)*]
    [you *(yourself)*]

ex

exact
examination
examine
    examined
    examiner
    examining
example
except *(to exclude)*
    [accept *(to receive)*]
    exception
excerpt
exchange
    exchanged
    exchanging
excite
    excited
    exciting
    excitement
exclaim
exclude
excuse
    excused
    excusing
exercise
    exercised
    exercising
exert
    exertion
exhausted
    exhausting
    exhaustion
exhibit
    exhibitor
    exhibition
exist
    existence
exit

expand
    expansion
expect
    expectation
expedition
expense
    expensive
experience
    experienced
    experiencing
experiment
    experimental
expert
explain
    explanation
explode
explore
    exploration
    explored
    explorer
    exploring
express
    expresses
    expression
extend
extra
extraordinary
extreme

ey

eye *(organ of sight)*
    [aye *(yes)*]
    [I *(myself)*]
    eyed
eyeball
eyelet *(small hole)*
    [islet *(small island)*]

fa

fable
fabric
fabulous
face
    faced
    facing
fact

factor
factory
   factories
fail
faint *(weak)*
   [feint *(false attack)*]
fair *(1. honest, 2. a bazaar)*
   [fare *(cost of ticket)*]
fairy *(an imaginary being)*
   [ferry *(a river-crossing boat)*]
   fairies
faith
fall *(irreg. vb)*
fallen
fallible
false
familiar
family
   families
fan
   fanned
   fanning
fancy
   fancied
   fancier
   fancies
   fanciest
fantastic
far
fare *(cost of ticket)*
   [fair *(1. honest, 2. a bazaar)*]
farm
farther *(greater physical distance)*
   [further *(greater extent)*]
fascinate
   fascination
fashion
   fashionable
fast
fasten
fat
   fatter
   fattest

father
fault
favor
   favorable
   favorite
faze *(upset)*
   [phase *(a stage)*]

fe

fear
feast
feat *(accomplishment)*
   [feet *(plural of foot)*]
feather
feature
   featured
   featuring
February
fed
federal
feed *(irreg. vb)*
feel
feet *(plural of foot)*
   [feat *(accomplishment)*]
feint *(false attack)*
   [faint *(weak)*]
fell
fellow
felt
female
fence
   fenced
   fencing
ferry *(a river-crossing boat)*
   [fairy *(an imaginary being)*]
fertile
   fertility
festival
festive
fever
few

fi

fiber
field
fierce
   fiercer
   fiercest
fifteen
   fifteenth
fifth
fifty
   fifties
   fiftieth
fig
fight
figure
   figured
   figuring
file
   filed
   filing
fill
film
filmstrip
final
find *(discover)* *(irreg. vb)*
   [fined *(forced to pay money as punishment)*]
fine
   fined *(forced to pay money as punishment)*
   [find *(discover)*]
   finer
   finest
   fining
finger
finish
   finishes
Finland
fir *(type of tree)*
   [fur *(animal hair)*]
fire
   fired
   firing

The following regular endings/suffixes are not in the word list but can be added to the root word without changes: -s, -ed, -ing, -er, -est, -ly, -ful, -less, and -ness. Most exceptions and root changes are in the list.

fireplace
firm
first
fish
  fishes
fisherman
  fishermen
fist
fit
  fitted
  fitting
five
  fifth
fix
  fixed
  fixes

fl

flag
  flagged
  flagging
flair *(natural talent)*
  [flare *(flaming signal)*]
flame
  flamed
  flaming
flammable
  flammability
flap
flare *(flaming signal)*
  [flair *(natural talent)*]
flash
  flashback
  flashcube
  flashes
  flashlight
flat
  flatten
flaunt
flavor
flea *(insect)*
  [flee *(run away)*]
flee *(run away) (irreg. vb)*
  [flea *(insect)*]
fleet
flew *(did fly)*
  [flu *(influenza)*]
  [flue *(chimney part)*]

flight
flip
float
flood
floor
floral
Florida
flotation
flour *(milled grain)*
  [flower *(blossom)*]
flow
flower *(blossom)*
  [flour *(milled grain)*]
flu *(influenza)*
  [flew *(did fly)*]
  [flue *(chimney part)*]
flute
  fluted
  fluting
fly *(irreg. vb)*
  flies

fo

fog
  fogging
  foggy
fold
folk
folklore
follow
food
fool
  foolish
foot
football
for *(in favor of)*
  [fore *(front part)*]
  [four *(the number 4)*]
forbid *(irreg. vb)*
  forbade
force
  forced
  forcing
ford
fore *(front part)*
  [for *(in favor of)*]
  [four *(the number 4)*]
forehead

foreign
forest
forever
foreword *(a preface)*
  [forward *(toward the front)*]
forgave
forget *(irreg. vb)*
  forgettable
  forgetting
forgot
  forgotten
fork
form
formal
  formally *(adjective)*
  [formerly *(adverb)*]
formation
former
  formerly *(adverb)*
  [formally *(adjective)*]
formula
fort
forth *(forward)*
  [fourth *(after third)*]
fortune
  fortunate
forty
  forties
  fortieth
forward *(toward the front)*
  [foreword *(a preface)*]
fossil
fought
foul *(bad)*
  [fowl *(a bird)*]
found
four *(the number 4)*
  [for *(in favor of)*]
  [fore *(front part)*]
  fourth *(after third)*
  [forth *(forward)*]
fourteen
  fourteenth
fowl *(a bird)*
  [foul *(bad)*]
fox
  foxes

fr

fraction
  fractional
frame
  framed
  framing
franc *(French money)*
  [frank *(honest)*]
France
frank *(honest)*
  [franc *(French money)*]
free
  freed
  freer
  freest
freedom
freeze *(irreg. vb)*
  freezing
French
frequent
  frequencies
  frequency
fresh
  freshen
friar *(member of religious order)*
  [fryer *(fryer chicken)*]
Friday
friend
  friendlier
  friendliest
  friendly
fright
  frighten
frog
frogman
from
front
frontier
frost
frostbite
froze
  frozen
fruit

fruitcake
fry
  fried
fryer *(frying chicken)*
  [friar *(member of religious order)*]

fu

fuel
full
fun
function
funny
  funnier
  funniest
fur *(animal hair)*
  [fir *(type of tree)*]
furnace
furniture
further *(greater extent)*
  [farther *(greater physical distance)*]
future

ga

gaiety
gain
gait *(pace)*
  [gate *(fence opening)*]
gallon
game
gang
garage
garden
garment
gas
  gases
gasoline
gate *(fence opening)*
  [gait *(pace)*]
gather
gauge
  gauged
  gauges

gave
gay

ge

gear
gene
general
generation
generous
genius
gentle
  gentler
  gently
gentleman
  gentlemen
geography
  geographies
geology
geometry
  geometric
  geometrically
  geometries
Georgia
germ
German
  Germany
get *(irreg. vb)*
  getting

gh

ghastly
ghetto
ghost
ghoul

gi

giant
gift
gilt *(golden)*
  [guilt *(opposite of innocence)*]
girl
give *(irreg. vb)*
  giver
  giving

The following regular endings/suffixes are not in the word list but can be added to the root word without changes: -s, -ed, -ing, -er, -est, -ly, -ful, -less, and -ness. Most exceptions and root changes are in the list.

gl

glacial
glacier
glad
   gladder
   gladdest
glance
   glanced
   glancing
glass
   glasses
   glassy
glee
glimpse
glint
globe
   global
glory
   glories
   glorious
glow
glue
   glued
   gluing

gn

gnu *(antelope)*
   [knew *(did know)*]
   [new *(opposite of old)*]

go

go *(irreg. vb)*
   goes
goal
goat
god
gold
   golden
goldenrod
goldfish
gone
good
good-bye
goose
gorilla *(type of ape)*
   [guerrilla *(irregular soldier)*]

got
government
   governmental
governor

gr

grab
   grabbed
   grabbing
grace
grade
   graded
   grading
gradual
grain
grammar
grand
grandfather
grandmother
grant
grape
graph
grass
   grasses
grasshopper
grassland
grate *(to grind)*
   [great *(1. large, 2. excellent)*]
grave
gravity
   gravities
gray
graze
   grazed
   grazing
great *(1. large, 2. excellent)*
   [grate *(to grind)*]
Great Britain
Greece
   Greek
greed
green
greet
grew
grief

grieve
   grievance
   grieved
   grieving
grin
   grinned
   grinning
grind *(irreg. vb)*
grip
groan *(moan)*
   [grown *(mature; adult)*]
grocery
   groceries
ground
group
grow *(irreg. vb)*
grown *(mature; adult)*
   [groan *(moan)*]
growth

gu

guard
Guatemala
guerrilla *(irregular soldier)*
   [gorilla *(type of ape)*]
guess
guest *(visitor)*
   [guessed *(surmised)*]
guide
   guidance
   guided
   guiding
guilt *(opposite of innocence)*
   [gilt *(golden)*]
   guilty
guitar
   guitarist
gulf
gum
gun
   gunned
   gunner
   gunning
guy

ha

habit
   habitual
habitat
had
hadn't *(had not)*
hail *(frozen rain)*
   [hale *(healthy)*]
hair *(growth on head)*
   [hare *(type of rabbit)*]
haircut
Haiti
hale *(healthy)*
   [hail *(frozen rain)*]
half
halfway
hall *(passage between rooms)*
   [haul *(carry)*]
halve *(cut in half)*
   [have *(possess)*]
hammer
hand
handcuff
handicap
handle
   handled
   handling
handlebar
handsome
   handsomer
   handsomest
handwriting
hang
hangar *(storage building)*
   [hanger *(tool for draping clothing)*]
hangup
happen
happy
   happier
   happiest
   happily
   happiness
harass
   harassment
harbor

hard
hardware
hardy
   hardier
   hardily
hare *(type of rabbit)*
   [hair *(growth on head)*]
harm
harmony
   harmonious
harness
   harnesses
harsh
harvest
has
hat
   hatter
hatch
   hatches
hate
   hated
   hating
haul *(carry)*
   [hall *(passage between rooms)*]
have *(possess)*
   [halve *(cut in half)*]
   having
haven't *(have not)*
Hawaii
   Hawaiian
hawk
hay *(dried grass)*
   [hey *(expression to get someone's attention)*]
haystack

he

he
head
headache
headlight
headquarters
heal *(make well)*
   [heel *(back part of foot)*]
   [he'll *(he will)*]

health
   healthier
   healthiest
   healthily
   healthy
hear *(listen) (irreg. vb)*
   [here *(this place)*]
heard *(listened)*
   [herd *(group of animals)*]
heart
heat
heaven
heavy
   heavier
   heaviest
   heavily
   heaviness
he'd *(he would)*
   [heed *(pay attention to)*]
heel *(back part of foot)*
   [heal *(make well)*]
   [he'll *(he will)*]
   heeled
height
heir *(successor)*
   [air *(what you breathe)*]
held
helicopter
he'll *(he will)*
   [heal *(make well)*]
   [heel *(back part of foot)*]
hello
helmet
help
hemisphere
hen
her
herd *(group of animals)*
   [heard *(listened)*]
here *(this place)*
   [hear *(listen)*]
hero
   heroes
   heroic
   heroine
herself
hew *(chop)*
   [hue *(a shade or color)*]

The following regular endings/suffixes are not in the word list but can be added to the root word without changes: -s, -ed, -ing, -er, -est, -ly, -ful, -less, and -ness. Most exceptions and root changes are in the list.

hey *(expression to get somone's attention)*
    [hay *(dried grass)*]

hi

hi *(word of greeting)*
    [high *(elevated)*]
hid
    hidden
hide *(irreg. vb)*
    hiding
high *(elevated)*
    [hi *(word of greeting)*]
highland
highway
hill
him *(that man or boy)*
    [hymn *(religious song)*]
himself
hip
hire *(employ)*
    [higher *(above)*]
his
Hispanic
history
    histories
hit
    hitter
    hitting

ho

hoard *(hidden supply)*
    [horde *(a crowd)*]
hoarse *(sounding rough and deep)*
    [horse *(type of animal)*]
hog
hold *(irreg. vb)*
holdup
hole *(an opening)*
    [whole *(complete)*]
holey *(full of holes)*
    [holy *(sacred)*]
    [wholly *(completely)*]
home
    homemade
    homeward
    homey

homonym
Honduras
honest
    honesty
Honolulu
honor
    honorable
hook
hop
    hopped
    hopping
hope
    hoped
    hoping
horde *(a crowd)*
    [hoard *(hidden supply)*]
horizon
    horizontal
horn
horse *(type of animal)*
    [hoarse *(sounding rough and deep)*]
hospitable
    hospitality
hospital
    hospitalize
hostel *(inn for young travelers)*
    [hostile *(unfriendly)*]
hot
    hotter
    hottest
hotel
hour *(sixty-minute period)*
    [our *(belonging to us)*]
house
    housed
    housing
Houston
how
however
howl

hu

hue *(a shade or color)*
    [hew *(chop)*]
huge

human
    humanism
    humanitarian
    humanity
    humanize
    humankind
    humanoid
humor
hump
hundred
hung
Hungary
hunger
hungry
    hungrier
    hungriest
    hungrily
hunt
hurry
    hurried
    hurriedly
hurt

hy

hydrogen
hymn *(religious song)*
    [him *(that man or boy)*]
hypocrite

i

I *(myself)*
    [aye *(yes)*]
    [eye *(organ of sight)*]

ic

ice
    iced
    icing
Iceland
icicle

id

I'd *(I would)*
Idaho
idea

ideal
identify
   identifies
identity
   identities
idle *(lazy)*
   [idol *(object of worship)*]

if

if

ig

ignite
   ignited
   igniting
ignition
ignore
   ignorance
   ignorant

il

ill
I'll *(I will)*
   [aisle *(narrow path)*]
   [isle *(small island)*]
Illinois
illuminate
   illuminated
   illuminating
illustration

im

I'm *(I am)*
image
imagery
imagine
   imaginable
   imaginary
   imagination
   imagined
   imagining
immediate
   immediacy

immigrate *(come to a country to live)*
   [emigrate *(leave your country)*]
   immigrant
   immigrated
   immigrating
imminent *(threaten to occur at any moment)*
   [eminent *(famous, outstanding)*]
imply
   implied
   implies
important
   importance
impossible
   impossibility
   impossibly
impostor
impression
improve
   improved
   improving

in

in *(opposite of out)*
   [inn *(type of hotel)*]
inch
include
   included
   including
   inclusion
income
increase
   increased
   increasing
incredible
indeed
independent
   independence
index
India
   Indian
Indiana
Indianapolis

indicate
   indicated
   indicating
   indication
   indicative
individual
industry
   industrial
   industries
inert
   inertia
inevitable
   inevitability
   inevitably
infer
   inference
influence
   influenced
   influencing
   influential
influenza
information
   informative
initial
ink
inland
inn *(type of hotel)*
   [in *(opposite of out)*]
inner
innocent
insect
insert
inside
insist
   insistence
instance *(an example or a situation)*
   [instants *(very short periods of time)*]
instant
instead
instinct
instruct
   instruction
   instructive
   instructor

The following regular endings/suffixes are not in the word list but can be added to the root word without changes: -s, -ed, -ing, -er, -est, -ly, -ful, -less, and -ness. Most exceptions and root changes are in the list.

instrument
  instrumental
  instrumentation
insure *(to issue or obtain insurance)*
  [ensure *(to secure, guarantee)*]
  insurance
  insured
  insuring
intend
intense *(extreme)*
  [intents *(purposes)*]
  intensify
  intensity
  intensive
intention
  intentional
interest
interior
internal
international
interrupt
intersect
  intersected
  intersecting
  intersection
interval
interview
into
introduce
  introduced
  introducing
  introduction
invent
  invention
  inventor
investigate
  investigated
  investigating
  investigation
  investigative
  investigator
invisible
  invisibility
  invisibly
invite
  invitation
  invited
  inviting

involve
  involved
  involvement
  involving
invulnerable

io
Iowa

ir
Iran
Iraq
irate
Ireland
  Irish
iris
iron
irony
  ironic
  ironically

is
is *(irreg. vb)*
island
isle *(island)*
  [aisle *(narrow path)*]
  [I'll *(I will)*]
islet *(small island)*
  [eyelet *(small hole)*]
isn't *(is not)*
Israel
  Israeli
issue
  issued
  issuing

it
it
italic
Italy
  Italian
Item
  itemize
it's *(it is)*
  [its *(belonging to it)*]
itself

ja
jacket
Jacksonville
jail
  jailor
jam *(fruit jelly)*
  [jamb *(part of a door frame)*]
January
Japan
  Japanese
jar
  jarred
  jarring
jaw
jazz
  jazzier
  jazziest
  jazzy

je
jelly
jellyfish
jest
  jester
jet
  jetted
  jetting
jettison
jetty
  jetties
jewel

ji
jiggle
jigsaw
jingle
  jingled
  jingling
jinx
  jinxes

jo
job
jobholder
jobless
join
joint

joke
  joked
  joker
  joking
journal
journey
journeyman
joy

ju

judge
  judged
  judgment
  judging
juice
July
jump
June
jungle
junior
jury
just
justice
justify
  justifiable
  justification

ka

Kansas

ke

keep *(irreg. vb)*
kelp
Kentucky
kept
kernel *(a seed or grain)*
  [colonel *(military officer)*]
kettle
key
keynote
keypunch
keystone

ki

kick
kid
  kidded
  kidding
kill
kind
kindle
  kindled
  kindling
king
kingdom
kink
kitchen
kite
kitten

kn

knead *(mix with hands)*
  [need *(require)*]
knee
kneel *(irreg. vb)*
knew *(did know)*
  [gnu *(antelope)*]
  [new *(opposite of old)*]
knife
  knives
knight *(servant of a king)*
  [night *(evening)*]
knit *(weave with yarn)*
  [nit *(louse egg)*]
knock
knot *(tangle)*
  [not *(in no manner)*]
knothole
knotty *(full of tangles)*
  [naughty *(bad)*]
know *(familiar with) (irreg. vb)*
  [no *(expression of refusal)*]
knowledge
  knowledgeable
  knowledgeably
known

ko

Korea

la

label
labor
laboratory
  laboratories
lack
lad
ladder
lady
  ladies
laid
lain *(past participle of lie)*
  [lane *(narrow street or path)*]
lake
lamb *(baby sheep)*
  [lam *(to leave quickly)*]
land
landlady
landlord
landscape
lane *(narrow street or path)*
  [lain *(past participle of lie)*]
language
lap
  lapped
  lapping
large
  larger
  largest
last
late
  later
  latest
Latin
latitude
  latitudinal

The following regular endings/suffixes are not in the word list but can be added to the root word without changes: -s, -ed, -ing, -er, -est, -ly, -ful, -less, and -ness. Most exceptions and root changes are in the list.

latter
laugh
   laughable
   laughter
law
lawn
lay *(past tense of lie) (irreg. vb)*
   [lei *(flower necklace)*]
layer
lazy
   lazier
   laziest
   lazily
   laziness

le

lead *(noun: a metal)*
   [led *(guided)*]
lead *(verb: to guide) (irreg. vb)*
leaf
   leaves
league
leak *(to drip)*
   [leek *(a vegetable)*]
lean *(1. slender, 2. slant
   to the side)*
   [lien *(a legal claim)*]
leap *(irreg. vb)*
learn
lease
leased *(rented)*
   [least *(smallest)*]
least *(smallest)*
   [leased *(rented)*]
leather
leave
leaving
led *(guided)*
   [lead *(a metal)*]
leek *(a vegetable)*
   [leak *(to drip)*]
left
leftover
leg
legal
   legality
   legalize

legend
   legendary
leg
lei *(flower necklace)*
   [lay *(past tense of lie)*]
leisure
lend *(irreg. vb)*
length
lens
   lenses
less
lesser *(of less size)*
   [lessor *(one who rents
   property)*]
lesson *(instruction)*
   [lessen *(make less)*]
lessor *(one who rents
   property)*
   [lesser *(of less size)*]
let
   letting
let's *(let us)*
letter
levee *(embankment)*
   [levy *(impose a tax)*]
level
lever
levy *(impose a tax)*
   [levee *(an embankment)*]

li

liable
liar
liberal
   liberalism
   liberalize
liberate
   liberation
Liberia
liberty
   liberties
library
   libraries
license
lichen *(fungus)*
   [liken *(compare)*]
lick
lid

lie *(1. falsify, 2. present
   tense of verb meaning "to get
   in a prone position") (irreg.vb)*
   [lye *(alkaline solution)*]
   lying
lien *(a legal claim)*
   [lean *(1. slender, 2. slant to
   the side)*]
lieu *(instead of)*
   [Lou *(a name)*]
life
lifeboat
lifeguard
lifelike
lifeline
lifetime
lifework
lift
light *(irreg. vb)*
lightning
like
   liked
   liken *(compare)*
   [lichen *(fungus)*]
   liking
limb
limit
   limitation
line
   lined
   lining
link
   linkage
lion
lip
lipstick
liquid
liquor
list
listen
literal
literate
   literacy
literature
little
   littler
   littlest

live
    lived
    livelier
    liveliest
    liveliness
    lively
    living
lizard

lo

load *(burden)*
    [lode *(vein of ore)*]
loaf
    loaves
loan *(something borrowed)*
    [lone *(single)*]
loathe
local
locate
    located
    locating
    location
lock
lode *(vein of ore)*
    [load *(burden)*]
log
    logged
    logger
    logging
logic
    logical
London
    Londoner
lone *(single)*
    [loan *(something borrowed)*]
    lonelier
    loneliest
long
longitude
look
lookout
loop

loose *(not fastened or restrained)*
    [lose *(to come to be without)*]
    looser
    loosest
loot *(steal)*
    [lute *(stringed musical instrument)*]
lord
Los Angeles
lose *(to come to be without) (irreg. vb)*
    [loose *(not fastened or restrained)*]
    loser
    losing
loss
    losses
lost
lot
Lou *(a name)*
    [lieu *(instead of)*]
Louisiana
loud
loudspeaker
love
    loved
    lover
    loving
lovely
    lovelier
    loveliest
    loveliness
low
lowland

lu

luck
    luckless
lucky
    luckier
    luckiest
    luckily
lumber
lump

lunch
    lunches
lung
lute *(stringed musical instrument)*
    [loot *(steal)*]
Luxembourg

ly

lye *(alkaline solution)*
    [lie *(falsify)*]

ma

Ma
machine
    machined
mad
    madder
    maddest
made *(manufactured)*
    [maid *(domestic servant)*]
magazine
magic
magnate *(person of power)*
    [magnet *(metal that attracts other metals)*]
magnet *(metal that attracts other metals)*
    [magnate *(person of power)*]
    magnetic
maid *(domestic servant)*
    [made *(manufactured)*]
mail *(send by post)*
    [male *(man or boy)*]
main *(most important)*
    [Maine *(a state)*]
    [mane *(horse's neck hair)*]
Maine *(a state)*
    [main *(most important)*]
    [mane *(horse's neck hair)*]
maintain
    maintenance
maize *(Native American corn)*
    [maze *(confusing network of paths)*]

The following regular endings/suffixes are not in the word list but can be added to the root word without changes: -s, -ed, -ing, -er, -est, -ly, -ful, -less, and -ness. Most exceptions and root changes are in the list.

major
   majority
   majorities
make
   maker
   making
male *(man or boy)*
   [mail *(send by post)*]
mall *(courtyard)*
   [maul *(mangle)*]
Mama
mammal
   mammalian
man
   manned
   manning
manage
   manageable
   managed
   management
   manager
   managing
mane *(horse's neck hair)*
   [main *(most important)*]
   [Maine *(a state)*]
manner *(way of behaving)*
   [manor *(mansion)*]
   mannered
mantel *(shelf over fireplace)*
   [mantle *(cloak)*]
manufacture
   manufactured
   manufacturer
   manufacturing
many
map
   mapped
   mapping
maple
marble
   marbled
march *(to walk)*
   [March *(month)*]
   marches
margin
   marginal
mark
market
   marketable
marriage
   marriageable

marry
   married
Mars
marshal *(law officer)*
   [martial *(warlike)*]
Maryland
mask
mass
   massed *(grouped)*
   [mast *(tall, straight pole)*]
   masses
Massachusetts
mast *(tall, straight pole)*
   [massed *(grouped)*]
master
mat
match
   matches
mate
   mated
   mating
material
   materialism
   materialize
mathematical
matter
maul *(mangle)*
   [mall *(courtyard)*]
may *(requesting or granting of permission)*
   [May *(the month)*]
May *(the month)*
   [may *(requesting or granting permission)*]
maybe
mayor
maze *(confusing network of paths)*
   [maize *(Native American corn)*]

me

me
meadow
meal
mean *(irreg. vb)*
meander
meaning
meantime
meanwhile

measure
   measured
   measurement
   measuring
meat *(animal flesh)*
   [meet *(greet)*]
   [mete *(deal out)*]
mechanic
   mechanical
medal *(an award)*
   [meddle *(interfere)*]
medicine
   medical
medieval
Mediterranean
medium
meek
meet *(greet)*
   [meat *(animal flesh)*]
   [mete *(deal out)*]
   meeting
melody
   melodic
melt
member
memento
memoir
memories
   memorable
Memphis
men
mental
   mentality
mention
   mentionable
merchant
mercury
mercy
mere
merry
   merrier
   merriest
   merrily
   merriment
mess
   messy
message
messenger
met

metal *(iron, gold, etc.)*
  [mettle *(courage)*]
  metallic
mete *(to deal out)*
  [meat *(animal flesh)*]
  [meet *(to greet)*]
meter
  metric
method
  methodical
  methodology
mettle *(courage)*
  [metal *(iron, gold, etc.)*]
Mexico
  Mexican

mi

mice
Michigan
microscope
  microscopic
middle
midnight
might *(1. may, 2. strength)*
  [mite *(small insect)*]
  mightier
  mightiest
  mightily
  mighty
mild
mile
mileage
military
milk
  milked
  milker
  milking
mill
  milled
  miller
  milling
million
Milwaukee
mind *(intellect)*
  [mined *(past tense of mine)*]

mine
  mined *(past tense of mine)*
  [mind *(intellect)*]
  miner *(coal digger)*
  [minor *(a juvenile)*]
  mining
mineral
mingle
  mingled
  mingling
miniature
minimum
  minimal
  minimize
ministry
Minnesota
minor *(a juvenile)*
  [miner *(coal digger)*]
minority
minus
minute
mirror
mischief
  mischievous
misconduct
misdemeanor
miserable
misery
misfortune
miss
  missed *(did not contact)*
  [mist *(fog)*]
  misses
  missing
Mississippi
Missouri
misspell
mist *(fog)*
  [missed *(did not contact)*]
mistake
  mistakable
  mistaken
  mistaking
  mistook
mister *(Mr.)*
mite *(small insect)*
  [might *(1. may, 2. strength)*]
mix
  mixes
  mixture

mo

moan *(groan)*
  [mown *(cut down)*]
mob
mobile
  mobility
mode *(the fashion)*
  [mowed *(cut down)*]
model
modem
modern
modify
  modifier
moist
  moisten
  moisture
mold
molecule
Mom
moment
  momentarily
  momentary
  momentous
  momentum
Monday
monetary
money
monkey
monotony
  monotonous
monster
  monstrosity
  monstrous
Montana
month
mood
  moodier
  moodiest
  moody
moon
  moonlight
  moonlike
  moonscape
  moonship
  moonwalk
moral *(concerned with right conduct)*
  [morale *(state of mind regarding cheerfulness)*]

The following regular endings/suffixes are not in the word list but can be added to the root word without changes: -s, -ed, -ing, -er, -est, -ly, -ful, -less, and -ness. Most exceptions and root changes are in the list.

moralist
morality
more
moreover
morn *(morning)*
  [mourn *(to grieve)*]
  morning
mosquito
  mosquitoes
moss
  mosses
most
moth
mother
motion
motor
  motorist
  motorcycle
mount
mountain
  mountaineer
  mountainous
  mountaintop
mourn *(to grieve)*
  [morn *(morning)*]
mouse
mouth
move
  movable
  moved
  movement
  moving
movie
  moviegoer
  moviemaker
mow *(irreg. vb)*
  mowed *(cut down)*
  [mode *(the fashion)*]
  mown *(cut down)*
  [moan *(groan)*]

mu

much
mud
mug
  mugger
  mugging
mule
mull

multiple
multiply
  multiplication
multitude
mumble
mummy
murder
  murderer
  murderous
murmur
muscle *(part of the body)*
  [mussel *(shellfish)*]
museum
music
  musical
  musician
must
mustache
musty
  mustier
  mustiest
  mustiness
mutual

my

my
myself
mystery
  mysteries
  mysterious
  mysteriously
mystic
  mystical
myth
  mythical
  mythology

na

nail
name
  named
  naming
narrow
nation
  national
  nationalism
  nationalistic
  nationality

native
natural
nature
naughty *(bad)*
  [knotty *(full of tangles)*]
navy
  naval *(nautical)*
  [navel *(depression in stomach)*]
  navies
nay *(no)*
  [neigh *(horse's whinnying sound)*]

ne

near
nearby
neat
Nebraska
necessary
  necessarily
necessity
neck
need *(require)*
  [knead *(mix with hands)*]
  needy
needle
  needled
  needling
negative
  negativity
neigh *(horse's whinnying sound)*
  [nay *(no)*]
neighbor
  neighborhood
  neighborly
neither
nerve
  nervous
nest
net
  netted
  netting
Netherland
  Netherlander
Nevada
never
nevertheless

new (*opposite of old*)
   [gnu (*antelope*)]
   [knew (*did know*)]
New Hampshire
New Jersey
New Mexico
New Orleans
newsboy
newscast
newspaper
newsprint
New York
New Zealand
next

ni

nice
   nicer
   nicest
niche
nickel
niece
night (*evening*)
   [knight (*servant of a king*)]
nightgown
nine
   ninth
nineteen
   nineteenth
ninety
   nineties
   ninetieth
ninth
nit (*louse egg*)
   [knit (*weave with yarn*)]

no

no (*expression of refusal*)
   [know (*to be familiar with*)]
noble
   nobility
   nobly
nobody
   nobodies
nod
   nodded
   nodding

noise
   noisier
   noisiest
   noisily
   noisy
none (*not any*)
   [nun (*woman living under vows of a religious order*)]
nonsense
noon
noonday
noontime
nor
normal
   normality
   normally
north
   northern
North Carolina
North Dakota
northeast
   northeastern
northwest
   northwestern
Norway
   Norwegian
nose
   nosed
   nosing
nostalgia
   nostalgic
   nostalgically
not (*in no manner*)
   [knot (*tangle*)]
note
   notable
   notation
notebook
nothing
notice
   noticeable
notion
notorious
noun
nourish
   nourishment
November
now
nowhere

nu

nuclear
number
   numbered
   numbering
numeral
numerator
numerous
nun (*woman living under vows of a religious order*)
   [none (*not any*)]
nurse
   nursed
   nursing
nut
nutcracker
nutrient
   nutrition
   nutritious

oa

oak
oar (*paddle for a boat*)
   [or (*word used to show choices*)]
   [ore (*mineral deposit*)]
oat
oatmeal

ob

obey
   obedience
   obedient
object
   objectify
   objection
   objective
obligate
   obligation
   obligatory
oblige
oblong
observe
   observable
   observant
   observation
   observatory
obtain
obvious

The following regular endings/suffixes are not in the word list but can be added to the root word without changes: -s, -ed, -ing, -er, -est, -ly, -ful, -less, and -ness. Most exceptions and root changes are in the list.

oc

occasion
   occasionally
occupy
   occupied
   occupies
occur
   occurred
   occurrence
   occurring
ocean
o'clock *(of the clock)*
October

od

odd
ode *(poem)*
   [owed *(did owe)*]
odor

of

of *(preposition)*
   [off *(adverb)*]
offal *(entrails)*
   [awful *(terrible)*]
offbeat
offer
office
   officer
   official
offshore
often

oh

oh *(an exclamation)*
   [owe *(be indebted)*]
Ohio

oi

oil
oilcan
oilcloth

ok

Oklahoma

ol

old
olive

olympiad
Olympic

om

omit
   omitted
   omitting

on

on
once
one *(the number 1)*
   [won *(triumphed)*]
ongoing
onion
only
onshore
onstage
onto
onward

op

open
opera
operate
   operation
   operational
   operator
opinion
   opinionated
opportune
   opportunist
   opportunity
   opportunities
oppose
   opposite
   opposition
oppress
   oppression
   oppressive
option
   optional
   optionally

or

or *(word used to show choices)*
   [oar *(paddle for a boat)*]
   [ore *(mineral deposit)*]
Oregon
organ

organism
organize
   organization
origin
   original
   originality
   originate

ot

other
otherwise

ou

ought
ounce
our *(belonging to us)*
   [hour *(sixty-minute period)*]
ourselves
out
outboard
outcome
outdoors
outer
outfield
outfit
outlaws
outline
   outlined
   outlining
outside
outstanding

ov

oven
over
overall
overboard
overcoat
overcome
   overcame
   overcoming
overdo *(go to extremes)*
   [overdue *(a bill not paid on time)*]
overhead
overhear
overlap
overlay
overlook
overnight

overpass
overpower
overseas *(abroad)*
  [oversees *(supervises)*]

ow

owe *(be indebted)*
  [oh *(an exclamation)*]
owed *(did owe)*
  [ode *(poem)*]
owl
own

ox

ox
  oxen
oxygen
  oxygenate

oy

oyster

oz

ozone

pa

Pa
pace
Pacific
pack
  packed *(did pack)*
  [pact *(agreement)*]
package
pact *(agreement)*
  [packed *(did pack)*]
pad
paddle
page
paid
pail *(bucket)*
  [pale *(light in color)*]
pain
  [pane *(window glass)*]
  pained
painstakingly

paint
pair *(two of a kind)*
  [pare *(to peel)*]
  [pear *(a fruit)*]
Pakistan
palace
palate *(roof of mouth)*
  [palette *(board that holds artist's paint)*]
  [pallet *(shovel-like tool)*]
pale *(light in color)*
  [pail *(bucket)*]
palette *(board that holds artist's paint)*
  [palate *(roof of mouth)*]
  [pallet *(shovel-like tool)*]
palm
pan
Panama
pancake
pane *(window glass)*
  [pain *(discomfort)*]
pants
Papa
paper
paperback
parade
  paraded
  parading
paragraph
Paraguay
parallel
  parallelogram
pare *(to peel)*
  [pair *(two of a kind)*]
  [pear *(a fruit)*]
parent
parenthesis
  parentheses
  parenthetic
Paris
park
parody
  parodied
parrot
part
partial

participate
  participation
  participator
  participatory
participle
particle
particular
partition
partner
party
  parties
pass
  passed *(moved by)*
  [past *(former time)*]
passage
passageway
passenger
passerby
  passersby
past *(former time)*
  [passed *(moved by)*]
paste
pasture
pat
patch
  patches
path
patience *(ability to endure)*
  [patients *(sick persons)*]
patient
  patients *(sick persons)*
  [patience *(ability to endure)*]
pattern
pause *(brief stop)*
  [paws *(feet of animals)*]
paw
  paws *(feet of animals)*
  [pause *(brief stop)*]
pay *(irreg. vb)*
payoff

pe

peace *(tranquility)*
  [piece *(part of a whole)*]
peach
  peaches

The following regular endings/suffixes are not in the word list but can be added to the root word without changes: -s, -ed, -ing, -er, -est, -ly, -ful, -less, and -ness. Most exceptions and root changes are in the list.

peak *(mountaintop)*
  [peek *(sneak a look)*]
  [pique *(spark interest)*]
peal *(ringing sound)*
  [peel *(skin or rind of fruit)*]
peanut
pear *(a fruit)*
  [pair *(two of a kind)*]
  [pare *(to peel)*]
pearl *(jewel)*
  [purl *(knitting stitch)*]
peculiar
pedal *(ride a bike)*
  [peddle *(sell)*]
peddle *(sell)*
  [pedal *(ride a bike)*]
peek *(sneak a look)*
  [peak *(mountaintop)*]
  [pique *(spark interest)*]
peel *(skin or rind of fruit)*
  [peal *(ringing sound)*]
peer *(an equal)*
  [pier *(a dock)*]
pen
pencil
peninsula
Pennsylvania
penny
  pennies
people
  peopled
pepper
peppermint
per *(for each)*
  [purr *(cat sound)*]
percent
  percentage
perfect
perform
  performance
perhaps
perimeter
period
  periodical
permanent
  permanence
permit
  permitted
  permitting

perpendicular
persecute
persevere
  perseverance
  persevered
  persevering
person
  personal *(of one person)*
  [personnel *(employees of a company)*]
personality
  personalities
personnel *(employees)*
  [personal *(of one person)*]
persuade
  persuaded
  persuading
Peru
pet
  petted
  petting

ph

phase *(a stage)*
  [faze *(upset)*]
Philadelphia
  Philadelphian
Philippines
Phoenix
photograph
  photographic
  photography
phrase
  phrased
  phrasing
physical
physician

pi

pi *(a letter in the Greek alphabet)*
  [pie *(type of pastry)*]
piano
  pianist
pick
  picked
  picking
picnic
  picnicked
  picnicker
  picnicking

picture
  pictured
  picturing
pie *(kind of pastry)*
  [pi *(a letter in the Greek alphabet)*]
piece *(part of a whole)*
  [peace *(tranquility)*]
  pieced
  piecing
pier *(a dock)*
  [peer *(an equal)*]
pig
pigeon
pigtail
pile
  piled
  piling
pilgrim
  pilgrimage
pilot
pin
  pinned
  pinning
pinball
pinch
pink
pinpoint
pioneer
pipe
  piped
  piping
pique *(spark interest)*
  [peak *(mountaintop)*]
  [peek *(sneak a look)*]
pirate
  piracy
  pirated
  pirating
pit
pitch
pity
  pitiable
  pitiably
  pitied
  pities
  pitiful
  pitiless

pl

place
  placed
  placing
plain *(not fancy)*
  [plane *(flat surface)*]
plaintive
plait *(braid)*
  [plate *(dish)*]
plan
  planned
  planner
  planning
plane *(flat surface)*
  [plain *(not fancy)*]
  planed
  planing
planet
  planetarium
  planetary
plant
plastic
  plasticity
plate *(dish)*
  [plait *(braid)*]
  plated
  plating
plateau
  plateaus *or*
  plateaux
platform
platitude
Plato
  platonic
platoon
play
playground
playmate
playpen
playwright
plaza
pleasant
please *(to make glad)*
  [pleas *(appeals)*]
pleasure
  pleasurable
plenty
  plentiful

plot
  plotted
  plotting
plow
plug
plum *(a fruit)*
  [plumb *(a lead weight)*]
plunder
plural
plus

po

pocket
poem
poet
  poetic
  poetry
poignant
point
  pointy
poise
  poised
poison
  poisonous
Poland
polar
pole *(a stick)*
  [poll *(an election)*]
  poled
  poling
police
  policed
  policing
policy
  policies
polish
polite
politics
  political
poll *(an election)*
  [pole *(a stick)*]
pollen
polyester
polygraph
pond
ponder
  ponderous

pony
  ponies
ponytail
pool
poor
pop
  popped
  popping
popcorn
popular
  popularity
population
porch
pore *(tiny opening in skin)*
  [pour *(to make liquid flow)*]
port
portion
portrait
portray
Portugal
pose
  posed
  poser
  posing
position
positive
possess
  possession
  possessive
possible
  possibility
  possibilities
  possibly
post
postcard
pot
  potted
  potter
  potting
potato
  potatoes
potent
potential
pottery
pound
pour *(to make liquid flow)*
  [pore *(tiny opening in skin)*]
powder
power

The following regular endings/suffixes are not in the word list but can be added to the root word without changes: -s, -ed, -ing, -er, -est, -ly, -ful, -less, and -ness. Most exceptions and root changes are in the list.

pr

pr

practical
practice
  practiced
  practicing
prairie
praise
  praised
  praising
praiseworthy
  praiseworthiness
pray *(worship)*
  [prey *(animal hunted for food)*]
  prayer
precede
  preceded
  preceding
precious
precise
predicate
  predicated
prefer
  preference
  preferential
  preferred
  preferring
prefix
  prefixes
prepare
  preparation
  prepared
  preparing
preposition
  prepositional
presence
present *(1. make a gift to, 2. stage a play or show)*
present *(1. the time now, 2. being in attendance)*
president
  presidential
press
pressure
  pressured
  pressuring
presume
  presumed
  presuming
  presumption

pretend
  pretense
  pretension
  pretentious
pretty
  prettied
  prettier
  pretties
  prettiest
  prettily
  prettiness
prevail
  prevalent
  prevalence
prevent
  prevention
previous
prey *(animal hunted for food)*
  [pray *(worship)*]
price
  priced
  pricing
prickly
  pricklier
  prickliest
  prickliness
pride *(self-esteem)*
  [pried *(1. inquired in a nosey way, 2. move with a level)*]
  prided
  priding
priest
  priestess
prim
primal
primary
  primaries
  primarily
primate
prime
  primed
  priming
primitive
prince
princess
  princesses
principal *(1. most important, 2. head of school)*
  [principle *(fundamental law)*]
print

prior
priority
  priorities
prison
pristine
private
privilege
  privileged
prize
probable
  probability
  probabilities
  probably
problem
  problematic
proceed
  procedure
process
prodigious
produce
  produced
  producer
  producing
product
  production
  productive
  productivity
profession
  professional
  professor
profit *(gain in money)*
  [prophet *(seer; visionary)*]
profound
program
  programmed
  programmer
  programming
progress *(1. gradual betterment, 2. to move forward)*
prohibit
  prohibitive
project
promise
  promised
  promising
promote
  promoted
  promoter
  promoting
pronoun

pronounce
    pronounced
    pronouncing
    pronunciation
proofread
propaganda
    propagandist
    propagandize
    propagandized
    propagandizing
propel
    propelled
    propeller
    propelling
proper
property
    properties
prophet *(seer; visionary)*
    [profit *(gain in money)*]
proportion
propose
    proposal
proposition
prose
prosecute
    prosecuted
    prosecuting
    prosecution
    prosecutor
prosper
    prosperity
    prosperous
protect
    protection
    protective
protein
proud
prove
    proved
    proven
    proving
provide
    provided
    providing
province
pry
    pried *(1. inquired in a nosey way, 2. moved with a lever)*
    [pride *(self-esteem)*]

ps

pseudonym
psychiatry
    psychiatric
    psychiatrist
psychology
    psychologist

pu

public
publicity
    publicist
publish
    publication
pull
pump
punctuate
punish
    punishment
pupil
puppy
    puppies
purchase
    purchased
    purchaser
    purchasing
pure
    purer
    purest
    purity
purl *(knitting stitch)*
    [pearl *(jewel)*]
purple
    purplish
purpose
purr *(cat sound)*
    [per *(for each)*]
pursue
    pursued
    pursuing
push
    pushes
pushover
put *(irreg. vb)*
    putting
puzzle
    puzzled
    puzzling

py

pyramid
pyre
python

qu

qualify
    qualified
    qualifies
quality
    qualities
quantity
    quantify
    quantities
quart
quarter
quarterback
quartet
quarts *(measure)*
    [quartz *(mineral)*]
queasy
    queasier
    queasiest
    queasiness
queen
queer
quench
    quenches
question
queue *(line of people)*
    [cue *(to prompt)*]
quick
    quicken
quicksand
quiet *(1. still, 2. silent)*
    [quite *(1. completely, 2. really)*]
quit
quite *(1. completely, 2. really)*
    [quiet *(1. still, 2. silent)*]
quiver
quiz
    quizzed
    quizzes
    quizzing
quizzical
    quizzically
quota

The following regular endings/suffixes are not in the word list but can be added to the root word without changes: -s, -ed, -ing, -er, -est, -ly, -ful, -less, and -ness. Most exceptions and root changes are in the list.

quote
 quotable
 quotation
 quoted
 quoting
quotient

ra

rabbi
rabbit
raccoon
race
 raced
 racer
 racing
radiation
radical
 radicalism
radio
radioactive
 radioactivity
radius
raft
rag
rage
 raged
 raging
rail
railroad
railway
rain *(precipitation)*
 [reign *(royal rule)*]
 [rein *(harness)*]
 rainier
 rainiest
 rainy
rainbow
rainfall
raise *(put up)*
 [raze *(tear down)*]
 [rays *(beams of energy)*]
 raised
 raising
rampant
 rampantly
ran *(irreg. vb)*
ranch
 rancher
 ranches
 ranching
rang
range
 ranged

ranger
ranging
rank
 ranked
 ranking
rap *(hit)*
 [wrap *(cover)*]
 rapped
 rapping
rapid
 rapidity
rare
 rarely
 rarer
 rarest
 rarity
rat
rate
 rated
 rater
 rating
rather
ratio
ration
rational
 rationalism
 rationalize
 rationally
rationale
rat
rattle
rattlesnake
raw
rawhide
ray
 rays *(beams of energy)*
 [raise *(put up)*]
 [raze *(tear down)*]

re

reach
 reaches
reaction
 reactionary
reactor
read *(scan printed matter)*
 (irreg. vb)
 [reed *(a plant)*]
 reader
 reading
read *(scanned printed matter)*
 [red *(a color)*]

ready
 readied
 readying
real *(genuine)*
 [reel *(spool)*]
 really
 realism
 reality
 realities
realize
 realization
 realized
 realizing
rear
 reared
 rearing
reason
 reasonable
 reasonably
rebel
 rebelled
 rebelling
 rebellion
 rebellious
recall
receipt
receive
 received
 receiver
 receiving
recent
receptacle
reception
 receptionist
receptive
recipe
recipient
reciprocal
reciprocate
 reciprocated
 reciprocating
recognize
 recognition
 recognizance
 recognized
 recognizing
recollect
 recollection
recommend
 recommendation
recompense
 recompensed
 recompensing

re (continued)

reconcile
  reconciled
  reconciliation
  reconciling
record
recover
rectangle
  rectangular
rectify
  rectified
  rectifies
  rectifying
red *(a color)*
  [read *(scanned printed matter)*]
  redder
  reddest
  redness
redwood
reduce
  reduced
  reducing
reed *(a plant)*
  [read *(scan printed matter)*]
reek *(give off strong odor)*
  [wreak *(inflict)*]
reel *(spool)*
  [real *(genuine)*]
refer
  referred
  referring
reference
referendum
  referenda
reflect
  reflection
  reflector
refrigerate
  refrigeration
  refrigerator
refuse
  refused
  refusing
regard
region
  regional
  regionalism
regret
  regrettable
  regretted
  regretting

regular
reign *(royal rule)*
  [rain *(precipitation)*]
  [rein *(harness)*]
relate
  related
  relating
relation
  relationship
relative
  relativism
  relativity
relax
  relaxation
release
  released
  releasing
relief
  relieve
  relieved
  relieving
religion
  religiosity
  religious
remain
  remainder
remarkable
  remarkably
remember
  remembrance
remind
reminisce
  reminiscence
  reminiscent
  reminiscing
remiss
  remission
remit
  remitted
  remitter
  remitting
remorse
remote
  remoter
  remotest
remove
  removable
  removed
  remover
  removing

rename
rendezvous
renounce
  renounced
  renouncing
  renunciation
rent
reorganize
  reorganization
  reorganized
  reorganizer
  reorganizing
repair
repeal
repeat
  repetition
  repetitious
repel
  repelled
  repellent
  repelling
repent
  repentance
  repentant
repercussion
repertoire
  repertory
repetition
  repetitious
replace
  replaceable
  replaced
  replacement
  replacing
replicate
  replicated
  replicating
  replication
reply
  replied
report
represent
  representation
  representative
reprieve
  reprieved
  reprieving
reproach

The following regular endings/suffixes are not in the word list but can be added to the root word without changes: -s, -ed, -ing, -er, -est, -ly, -ful, -less, and -ness. Most exceptions and root changes are in the list.

reptile
  reptilian
republic
  Republican
repudiate
  repudiated
  repudiating
  repudiation
repulse
  repulsed
  repulsing
  repulsion
reputation
repute
require
  required
  requiring
requirement
requisite
requisition
rescue
  rescued
  rescuer
  rescuing
research
resemble
  resemblance
  resembled
  resembling
resist
  resistance
  resistant
resolute
  resolution
resolve
  resolved
  resolving
resonant
  resonance
resource
respect
  respectability
  respectably
respectfully *(showing politeness)*
  [respectively *(in regard to each of a number in the order given)*]
respective
  respectively *(in regard to each of a number in the order given)*
  [respectfully *(showing politeness)*]

respond
responsible
  responsibilities
  responsibility
responsive
rest *(relax)*
  [wrest *(take from)*]
restaurant
  restaurateur
restless
result
  resultant
resume *(take up again)*
  resumed
  resuming
  resumption
resume *(short account of one's career)*
resurrect
  resurrection
retain
retaliate
retention
  retentive
reticent
  reticence
retinue
retire
retort
return
  returnable
reveal
revelation
reverend
review
revolt
revolution
  revolutionary
reward
rewrite
  rewriting
  rewritten
  rewrote

rh

Rhine River
rhinoceros
Rhode Island
rhyme *(repetition of same sounds)*
  [rime *(type of ice; frost)*]
  rhymed

rhymer
rhyming
rhythm
rhythmic
  rhythmical

ri

rib
  ribbed
  ribbing
ribbon
rice
rich
  riches
ride *(irreg. vb)*
  rider
  riding
ridge
ridicule
  ridiculous
rifle
  rifled
  rifling
right *(correct)*
  [rite *(ceremony)*]
  [write *(inscribe)*]
rigid
rime *(type of ice; frost)*
  [rhyme *(repetition of same sounds)*]
ring *(circular band)*
  [wring *(squeeze)*]
ring *(irreg. vb)*
rink
riot
rip
  ripped
  ripping
ripe
ripen
ripoff
rise *(irreg. vb)*
  rising
risk
  risky
rite *(ceremony)*
  [right *(correct)*]
  [write *(inscribe)*]

rival
rivalry
   rivalries
river

ro

road *(street)*
   [rode *(traveled)*]
   [rowed *(used oars)*]
roar
robot
   robotic
rock
   rocky
rocket
rode *(traveled)*
   [road *(street)*]
   [rowed *(used oars)*]
roe *(fish eggs)*
   [row *(1. a line, 2. use oars)*]
role *(a part played)*
   [roll *(1. turn over, 2. bread)*]
roll *(1. turn over, 2. bread)*
   [role *(a part played)*]
romance
   romanced
   romancing
   romantic
   romantically
Romania
Rome
   Roman
root *(part of a plant)*
   [route *(roadway)*]
   rooted
   rooter
   rooting
rope
   roped
   roper
   roping
rose *(type of flower)*
   [rows *(1. lines, 2. uses oars)*]
rote *(by memory)*
   [wrote *(did write)*]
rough *(not smooth)*
   [ruff *(pleated collar)*]

round
route *(roadway)*
   [root *(part of a plant)*]
   routed
   routing
row *(1. a line, 2. use oars)*
   [roe *(fish eggs)*]
   rowed *(used oars)*
   [road *(street)*]
   [rode *(traveled)*]
rowboat
royal

ru

rub
   rubbed
   rubbing
rubber
   rubbery
ruby
rude *(impolite)*
   rued *(regretted)*
rues *(regrets)*
   [ruse *(artful trick)*]
rug
rugged
rule
   ruled
   ruler
   ruling
rumor
run *(irreg. vb)*
   runner
   running
runaway
rung *(a step on a ladder)*
   [wrung *(squeezed)*]
runway
ruse *(artful trick)*
   [rues *(regrets)*]
rush
   rushes
Russia
   Russian
rust
   rusty

ry

rye *(grain)*
   [wry *(ironically humorous)*]

sa

sack
sacrifice
sad
   sadden
   sadder
   saddest
saddle
   saddled
   saddling
safe
   safer
   safest
safety
   safeties
said
sail *(travel by boat)*
   [sale *(selling at bargain prices)*]
sailboat
sailor
saint
salad
sale *(selling at bargain prices)*
   [sail *(travel by boat)*]
salmon
salt
   saltier
   saltiest
   salty
salute
   saluted
   saluting
Salvador
same
sample
   sampled
   sampler
   sampling
San Antonio
San Diego
sand
   sandy

The following regular endings/suffixes are not in the word list but can be added to the root word without changes: -s, -ed, -ing, -er, -est, -ly, -ful, -less, and -ness. Most exceptions and root changes are in the list.

sandal
sandpaper
sandwich
    sandwiches
San Francisco
sang
San Jose
sank
Santa Claus
sap
sash
sat
satellite
satin
satisfy
    satisfaction
    satisfactory
    satisfied
Saturday
sauce
    saucy
save
    saved
    saver
    saving
saw *(irreg. vb)*
say *(irreg. vb)*

sc

scale
    scaled
    scaling
scar
scarce
    scarcer
    scarcest
scarcity
scare
    scared
    scarier
    scariest
    scaring
    scary
scarecrow
scarf
    scarves
scatter
scene *(setting)*
    [seen *(viewed)*]

scent *(smell)*
    [cent *(penny)*]
    [sent *(did send)*]
schedule
    scheduled
    scheduling
scholar
    scholarly
    scholarship
school
science
scientific
    scientifically
scientist
scissor
scold
scoop
scoot
    scooter
scope
scorch
score
    scored
    scorer
    scores
    scoring
scout
scraggly
scramble
    scrambled
    scrambling
scrap
    scrapped
    scrapping
scratch
    scratches
    scratchy
scrawl
scrawny
    scrawnier
    scrawniest
scream
screech
screen
screenplay
screenwriter
screw
screwball
screwdriver
scribble
    scribbled
    scribbler
    scribbling

scrimp
script
scroll
scrub
    scrubbed
    scrubbier
    scrubbiest
    scrubbing
    scrubby
scruff
scuff
    scuffed
    scuffing
scull *(racing boat)*
    [skull *(the head)*]
sculptor
sculpture
    sculptured
    sculpturing
scum
    scummed
    scumming
scurry

se

sea *(ocean)*
    [see *(visualize)*]
seal
sealing *(closing)*
    [ceiling *(top of room)*]
seam *(where two pieces meet)*
    [seem *(give the impression of being)*]
    seamy
sear *(singe)*
    [seer *(prophet; visionary)*]
search
    searches
season
    seasonable
    seasonal
seat
Seattle
seaward
second
    secondary
secrecy
secret
    secretive
secretary
    secretarial
    secretaries

section
   sectional
secure
   secured
   securing
security
   securities
sedate
   sedated
   sedating
   sedative
see *(visualize) (irreg. vb)*
   [sea *(ocean)*]
seed *(part of a plant)*
   [cede *(give over; surrender)*]
seek *(irreg. vb)*
seem *(give the impression of being)*
   [seam *(where two pieces join)*]
seen *(viewed)*
   [scene *(setting)*]
seer *(prophet; visionary)*
   [sear *(singe)*]
segment
seize
   seized
   seizes
   seizing
   seizure
seldom
select
   selection
   selective
self
sell *(exchange for money)*
   (irreg. vb)
   [cell *(prison room)*]
   seller *(one who sells)*
   [cellar *(basement)*]
semester
senate
   senator
send *(irreg. vb)*
sent *(did send)*
   [cent *(penny)*]
   [scent *(odor)*]
senior
   seniority

sense *(feel)*
   [cents *(pennies)*]
   sensed
   senseless
   sensibility
   sensible
   sensibly
   sensing
sensitive
sensor *(detection device)*
   [censor *(ban)*]
   sensory
sent *(did send)*
   [cent *(penny)*]
   [scent *(smell)*]
sentence
   sentenced
   sentencing
separate
   separated
   separating
   separation
September
serf *(feudal servant)*
   [surf *(ocean waves)*]
sergeant
series
   serial *(of a series)*
   [cereal *(food made from grain)*]
serious
serpent
   serpentine
servant
serve
   served
   server
   serving
service
   serviced
   servicing
session *(a meeting)*
   [cession *(yielding)*]
set
setting

settle
   settled
   settlement
   settler
   settles
   settling
seven
   seventh
seventeen
   seventeenth
seventy
   seventies
   seventieth
several
severe
   severity
sew *(mend) (irreg. vb)*
   [so *(in order that)*]
   [sow *(plant seeds)*]
sewage
sewer
sewn

sh

shabby
   shabbier
   shabbiest
   shabbily
   shabbiness
shackle
   shackled
   shackling
shade
   shaded
   shadier
   shadiest
   shading
   shady
shadow
   shadowy
shaft
shake *(irreg. vb)*
   shaken
   shaker
   shakier
   shakiest
   shaking
   shaky

The following regular endings/suffixes are not in the word list but can be added to the root word without changes: -s, -ed, -ing, -er, -est, -ly, -ful, -less, and -ness. Most exceptions and root changes are in the list.

shall
shallow
shamble *(walk awkwardly
    or unsteadily)*
    shambled
    shambles *(confusion; a mess)*
    shambling
shame
    shamed
    shaming
shamefaced
shampoo
shape
    shaped
    shapeliest
    shaping
share
    shared
    sharer
    sharing
shark
sharp
shave
    shaved
    shaven
    shaver
    shaving
she
shear *(cut)*
    [sheer *(transparent)*]
shed
    shedding
she'd *(she had, she would)*
sheep
sheer *(transparent)*
    [shear *(cut)*]
sheet
sheik *(Arab chief)*
    [chic *(stylish)*]
shelf
    shelved
    shelves
    shelving
shell
she'll *(she will)*
shelter
shepherd
sheriff
she's *(she has, she is)*
shield

shift
    shiftier
    shiftiest
    shiftiness
    shifty
shine *(irreg. vb)*
    shinier
    shiniest
    shining
    shiny
ship
    shipped
    shipping
    shipwreck
shirt
shock
shoe *(foot covering)*
    [shoo *(chase away)*]
shoelace
shone *(beamed)*
    [shown *(exhibited)*]
shoo *(chase away)*
    [shoe *(foot covering)*]
shook *(irreg. vb)*
shoot *(discharge gun)*
    [chute *(slide)*]
shop
    shopped
    shopper
    shopping
shore
    shored
    shoring
short
shortstop
shot
shotgun
should
shoulder
shout
shovel
show *(irreg. vb)*
    showcase
    showcased
    showcasing
    shower
shown *(exhibited)*
    [shone *(beamed)*]
showroom
shrank
shred
shriek

shrill
shrink *(irreg. vb)*
    shrinkage
shrug
    shrugged
    shrugging
shrunk
shuffle
    shuffled
    shuffling
shut *(irreg. vb)*
    shutting
shy
    shier
    shiest

si

sick
    sicken
    sickening
side *(flank)*
    [sighed *(breathed audibly)*]
    sided
    siding
sidewalk
sideways
sigh
    sighed *(breathed audibly)*
    [side *(flank)*]
    sighing
    sighs *(audible breaths)*
    [size *(physical dimension)*]
sight *(vision)*
    [cite *(give credit to a source)*]
    [site *(location)*]
    sighted
    sighting
sign *(signal)*
    [sine *(trigonometric function)*]
signal
signature
significant
    significance
silent
    silence
    silenced
    silencer
    silencing
silk
    silken
    silky

silly
  sillier
  silliest
  silliness
silver
  silvery
silverware
similar
  similarities
  similarity
simile
simmer
simper
simple
  simpler
  simplest
  simply
simplicity
simplify
  simplified
  simplifies
  simplifying
simulate
  simulated
  simulating
  simulation
simultaneous
since
sine *(trigonometric function)*
  [sign *(signal)*]
sing *(irreg. vb)*
single
  singled
  singling
singular
  singularity
  singularities
sink *(irreg. vb)*
sip
  sipped
  sipping
sir
sister
sit *(irreg. vb)*
  sitter
  sitting
site *(location)*
  [cite *(give credit to a source)*]
  [sight *(vision)*]

situate
  situated
  situating
  situation
  situational
six
  sixes
  sixth
sixteen
  sixteenth
sixty
  sixties
  sixtieth
size *(physical dimension)*
  [sighs *(audible breaths)*]
  sized
  sizing

sk

skate
skateboard
skeleton
  skeletal
skeptic
  skeptical
  skepticism
sketch
ski
  skied
  skiing
skid
  skidded
  skidding
skill
skin
skip
  skipped
  skipper
  skipping
skirt
skull *(head)*
  [scull *(racing boat)*]
skunk
sky
  skies
skyscraper

sl

slack
  slacken
slam
  slammed
  slamming
slang
slant
slap
  slapped
  slapping
slave
  slaved
  slavery
  slaving
slay *(kill)*
  [sleigh *(sled)*]
sled
  sledded
  sledding
sleep *(irreg. vb)*
  sleepier
  sleepiest
  sleepily
  sleepiness
  sleepy
sleeve
sleigh *(sled)*
  [slay *(kill)*]
sleight *(skill)*
  [slight *(slender)*]
slept
slice
  sliced
  slicing
slid
slide *(irreg. vb)*
  slider
  sliding
slight *(slender)*
  [sleight *(skill)*]
slim
  slimmer
  slimmest
  slimming
slip
  slipped
  slippery
  slipping

The following regular endings/suffixes are not in the word list but can be added to the root word without changes: -s, -ed, -ing, -er, -est, -ly, -ful, -less, and -ness. Most exceptions and root changes are in the list.

slipcover
slope
   sloped
   sloping
sloppy
   sloppier
   sloppiest
slot
   slotted
   slotting
slow
slug
   slugged
   slugging
   sluggish
slumber
slump

sm

small
smart
   smarten
smash
smear
smell
   smellier
   smelliest
   smelly
smile
   smiled
   smiling
smoke
   smoked
   smoker
   smoking
   smoky
smooth
smother

sn

snack
snag
   snagged
   snagging
snake
   snaked
   snaking
snap
   snapped

snapping
snappy
sneak
sneeze
sniff
snip
   snipped
   snipping
   snippy
snore
   snored
   snoring
snow
   snowy
snowball
snowdrift
snowfall
snowflake
snowman
snowstorm
snub
   snubbed
   snubbing
snuggle

so

so *(in order that)*
   [sew *(mend)*]
   [sow *(plant seeds)*]
soak
soap
   soapy
soar *(fly)*
   [sore *(painful)*]
social
society
   societies
sock
soda
sofa
soft
softball
soil
sold *(did sell)*
   [soled *(bottom placed on a shoe)*]
sole *(1. only, 2. bottom)*
   [soul *(spirit)*]
solicit
   solicitor
solid

solution
solve
   solved
   solving
some *(a portion)*
   [sum *(total)*]
somebody
someday
somehow
someone
something
sometime *(indefinite, unspecified)*
   [sometimes *(on some occasions, now and then)*]
somewhat
somewhere
son *(male offspring)*
   [sun *(a star)*]
song
soon
sore *(painful)*
   [soar *(fly)*]
sorry
   sorrier
   sorriest
sort
sought
soul *(spirit)*
   [sole *(1. only, 2. bottom of foot)*]
sound
soup
sour
source
south
South Africa
South Carolina
South Dakota
southeast
   southeastern
southern
   southernmost
southwest
   southwestern
Soviet
sow *(plant seeds) (irreg. vb)*
   [sew *(mend)*]
   [so *(in order that)*]
   sown

sp

space
   spaced
   spacing
   spacious
Spain
   Spaniard
   Spanish
spare
   spared
   sparing
spark
spasm
speak *(irreg. vb)*
spear
special
species
specific
   specifically
specify
   specified
   specifies
speech
   speeches
speed
   sped, speeded
speedy
   speedier
   speediest
   speediness
spell
spend *(irreg. vb)*
   spent
sphere
spider
spill
   spilled, spilt
spin *(irreg. vb)*
   spinner
   spinning
spiral
spirit
spit *(irreg. vb)*
spite
splash
   splashes
splashdown
split *(irreg. vb)*
   splitting

spoil
   spoiled, spoilt
spoke *(1. did speak, 2. part of a wheel)*
   spoken
spoon
sport
   sports
spot
   spotted
   spotting
spotlight
sprang
spread *(irreg. vb)*
spring *(irreg. vb)*
sprinkle
sprung
spun

sq

square
   squared
   squaring
squeak
squeeze
   squeezed
   squeezing
squirm
squirrel
squirt

st

stab
   stabbed
   stabbing
stability
   stabilities
stabilize
   stabilized
   stabilizer
   stabilizing
stable
   stabler
   stablest
stack
stadium
staff
stage
   staged
   staging

staid *(proper)*
   [stayed *(remained)*]
stain
stair *(a step)*
   [stare *(look intently)*]
stake *(post)*
   [steak *(slice of beef)*]
stall
stamp
stand *(irreg. vb)*
standard
stanza
star
   starred
   starring
   starry
starboard
stardom
stardust
stare *(look intently)*
   [stair *(a step)*]
   stared
   staring
starfish
starry
   starrier
   starriest
start
state
   stated
   stating
statement
station
stationary *(in a fixed position)*
   [stationery *(writing paper)*]
statistic
   statistical
   statistically
   statistician
statue
stay
   stayed *(remained)*
   [staid *(proper)*]
steady
   steadied
   steadier
   steadies
   steadiest
   steadily
   steadiness

The following regular endings/suffixes are not in the word list but can be added to the root word without changes: -s, -ed, -ing, -er, -est, -ly, -ful, -less, and -ness. Most exceptions and root changes are in the list.

steak (*slice of beef*)
  [stake (*post*)]
steal (*rob*) (*irreg. vb*)
  [steel (*metal*)]
steam
  steamy
steel (*metal*)
  [steal (*rob*)]
steep
steeple
steer
stem
  stemmed
  stemming
step (*walk*)
  [steppe (*prairie of Europe or Asia*)]
  stepped
  stepping
stereo
stereotype
  stereotypical
stern
stick (*irreg. vb*)
  sticky
stiff
stile (*gate*)
  [style (*fashion*)]
still
sting
stir
  stirred
  stirring
stitch
  stitches
stock
  stocked
  stocking
stole
stolen
stomach
stone
  stoned
  stoning
stood
stop
  stopped
  stopper
  stopping

store
  stored
  storing
storm
  stormy
story
  stories
stove
straight (*not crooked*)
  [strait (*channel of water*)]
strain
strait (*channel of water*)
  [straight (*not crooked*)]
strange
  stranger
  strangest
strategy
  strategies
straw
streak
stream
streamline
  streamlined
  streamliner
street
streetcar
strength
  strengthen
stress
  stresses
  stressful
stretch
  stretches
stride (*irreg. vb*)
  striding
strike (*irreg. vb*)
  striker
  striking
string (*irreg. vb*)
strip
  stripped
  stripper
  stripping
strode
stroke
  stroked
  stroking
strong
struck
structure
  structured
  structuring

struggle
  struggled
  struggling
strung
stubborn
stuck
student
study
  studied
stuff
stung
stupid
style (*fashion*)
  [stile (*gate*)]
  styled
  styling

su

subject
submarine
  submariner
submerge
  submerged
  submerging
submerse
  submersed
  submersing
subset
substance
substitute
  substituted
  substituting
  substitution
subtle
  subtler
  subtlest
  subtleties
  subtlety
  subtly
subtract
  subtraction
succeed
success
  successes
succinct
succumb
such
sudden
sue

suffer
suffice
   sufficed
   sufficient
   sufficing
suffix
   suffixes
sugar
   sugary
suggest
   suggestion
   suggestive
suit
suitable
   suitability
   suitably
suitcase
suite *(connected rooms)*
   [sweet *(sugary)*]
sum *(total)*
   [some *(portion)*]
   summed
   summing
summer
sun *(star)*
   [son *(male offspring)*]
   sunned
   sunning
sunbeam
Sunday
sunflower
sung
sunk
sunlight
sunny
   sunnier
   sunniest
sunrise
sunset
sunshine
suntan
   suntanned
   suntanning
super
superficial
superior
supermarket

supersede
   superseded
   superseding
supervise
   supervision
   supervisor
   supervisory
supine
supper
supply
   supplied
   supplier
   supplies
support
suppose *(verb)*
   [supposed *(adjective)*]
   supposing
supreme
sure
   surer
   surest
surf *(ocean waves)*
   [serf *(feudal servant)*]
surface
   surfaced
   surfacing
surprise
   surprised
   surprising
surround
survey
   surveyor
survive
   survival
   survived
   surviving
   survivor
suspect

sw

swallow
swam
swamp
swear *(irreg. vb)*
sweat
sweater
sweatshirt

Swede
   Sweden
sweep
sweet *(sugary)*
   [suite *(connected rooms)*]
   sweeten
sweetheart
swell
swept
swift
swim *(irreg. vb)*
   swimmer
   swimming
swing *(irreg. vb)*
   swinger
   swinging
Swiss
   Switzerland
switch
   switches
sword
swore
sworn
swum
swung

sy

syllable
syllabication
symbol *(sign)*
   [cymbal *(percussion instrument)*]
sympathetic
   sympathetically
sympathy
   sympathies
   sympathize
symphony
   symphonies
symptom
   symptomatic
synagogue
synonym
   synonymous
Syria
system
   systematic
   systematically

The following regular endings/suffixes are not in the word list but can be added to the root word without changes: -s, -ed, -ing, -er, -est, -ly, -ful, -less, and -ness. Most exceptions and root changes are in the list.

ta

table
tacks *(flat-headed nails)*
   [tax *(money paid to government)*]
tag
   tagged
   tagging
tail *(animal's hind appendage)*
   [tale *(story)*]
   tailless
tailor
take *(irreg. vb)*
   taking
taken
tale *(story)*
   [tail *(animal's hind appendage)*]
talk
tall
tank
tap
   tapped
   tapping
tape
   taped
   taping
taps *(bugle call)*
tar
tardy
target
tart
task
taste
   tasted
   taster
   tasting
taught *(did teach)*
   [taut *(tight)*]
tax *(money paid to government)*
   [tacks *(flat-headed nails)*]
   taxes

te

tea *(a hot drink)*
   [tee *(holder for golf balls)*]
teach *(irreg. vb)*
   teaches
teacup
team *(crew)*
   [teem *(swarm)*]

tear *(water from eye)*
   [tier *(row)*]
tear *(irreg. vb)*
tease *(mock)*
   [teas *(hot drinks)*]
   [tees *(holders for golf balls)*]
teaspoon
technical
technique
tee *(holder for golf balls)*
   [tea *(a hot drink)*]
teem *(swarm)*
   [team *(crew)*]
teenage
   teenager
teeth
teetotal
telecast
telecommunication
telegram
   telegrammed
   telegramming
telephone
   telephoned
   telephoning
telescope
   telescoped
   telescoping
televise
   televised
   televising
   television
tell *(irreg. vb)*
temperament
   temperamental
temperature
temple
temporary
   temporarily
tempt
ten
   tenth
tenant
tend
tendency
   tendencies
tender
Tennessee
tense
   tensed
   tensing

tent
tenth
term
tern *(sea bird)*
   [turn *(rotate)*]
terrible
terrific
territory
   territorial
   territories
terror
test
Texas
textbook
texture
   textured
   texturing

th

than *(conjunction)*
   [then *(adverb)*]
thank
Thanksgiving
that
the
theater
   theatrical
thee
their *(belonging to them)*
   [there *(at that place)*]
   [they're *(they are)*]
theirs *(belonging to them)*
   [there's *(there is)*]
them
theme
themselves
then *(adverb)*
   [than *(conjunction)*]
theory
there *(at that place)*
   [their *(belonging to them)*]
   [they're *(they are)*]
therefore
there's *(there is)*
   [theirs *(belonging to them)*]
thermometer
thermonuclear
these
they

they'd *(they would)*
they'll *(they will)*
they're *(they are)*
    [their *(belonging to them)*]
    [there *(at that place)*]
thick
thief
thin
    thinned
    thinner
    thinness
    thinnest
    thinning
thing
think *(irreg. vb)*
third
thirsty
thirteen
    thirteenth
thirty
    thirties
    thirtieth
this
thorough
those
thou
though
thought
thousand
    thousandfold
    thousandth
thread
threat
three
threw *(tossed)*
    [through *(finished)*]
thrill
throat
throne *(king's chair)*
    [thrown *(tossed)*]
through *(finished)*
    [threw *(tossed)*]
throughout
throw *(irreg. vb)*
    thrown *(tossed)*
    [throne *(king's chair)*]
thrust
thumb
thumbtack
thunder

thunderstorm
Thursday
thus
thy
thyme *(herb)*
    [time *(past, present, and future)*]

ti

tic *(twitch)*
    [tick *(1. insect, 2. clock sound)*]
ticket
    ticketed
    ticketing
tickle
tide *(ebb and flow)*
    [tied *(bound)*]
tie
    tied *(bound)*
    [tide *(ebb and flow)*]
    tying
tier *(a row)*
    [tear *(water from eye)*]
tiger
tight
till
timber
time *(past, present, and future)*
    [thyme *(herb)*]
    timed
    timer
    timing
    timelier
    timeliest
    timeliness
    timely
timetable
timeworn
timid
    timidity
tin
    tinned
    tinning
tinder
tinderbox

tinfoil
tinge
    tinged
tiny
    tinier
    tiniest
tip
    tipped
    tipper
    tipping
tiptoe
tire
    tired
    tiredness
    tireless
    tiresome
    tiring
tissue
title
    titled
    titling

to

to *(toward)*
    [too *(also)*]
    [two *(the number 2)*]
toad *(froglike animal)*
    [towed *(pulled)*]
tobacco
today
toe *(digit on foot)*
    [tow *(pull)*]
toenail
together
    togetherness
told *(informed)*
    [tolled *(rang)*]
tomorrow
ton
tone
tongue
    tongued
    tonguing
tonic
tonight
too *(also)*
    [to *(toward)*]
    [two *(the number 2)*]

The following regular endings/suffixes are not in the word list but can be added to the root word without changes: -s, -ed, -ing, -er, -est, -ly, -ful, -less, and -ness. Most exceptions and root changes are in the list.

took
tool
tooth
toothbrush
toothpick
top
  topped
  topper
  topping
topic
topical
topple
  toppled
  toppling
tore
torn
torture
  tortured
  torturer
  torturing
toss
total
touch
  touches
  touchier
  touchiest
  touchy
touchdown
tough
tow *(pull)*
  [toe *(digit on foot)*]
toward
towed *(pulled)*
  [toad *(froglike animal)*]
tower
town
township
townspeople
toxic
  toxicity
toy

tr

trace
  traced
  tracer
  tracing
track
trade
  traded
  trader
  trading

tradition
  traditional
traffic
tragedy
  tragedies
tragic
  tragically
trail
train
transact
transatlantic
transform
translate
  translated
  translating
  translation
  translator
transportation
trap
  trapped
  trapper
  trapping
travel
tray
treasure
  treasured
  treasurer
  treasuring
treat
treatment
treaty
  treaties
tree
  treed
  treelike
treetop
tremendous
trial
triangle
tribe
trick
  trickery
  tricky
tried
trim
  trimmed
  trimmer
  trimming
trip
  tripped
  tripping

troop *(military)*
  [troupe *(acting)*]
tropical
trouble
  troubled
  troublesome
  troubling
troupe *(acting)*
  [troop *(military)*]
truck
true
  truer
  truest
  truly
trumpet
trunk
trust *(confidence)*
  [trussed *(tied up)*]
truth
try
  tried
  tries

tu

tub
tube
Tuesday
tug
tugboat
tumble
tune
  tuned
  tuning
tunnel
turkey
Turkey
turn *(rotate)*
  [tern *(sea bird)*]
turntable
turtle
turtleneck

tw

twelve
  twelfth
twenty
  twenties
  twentieth
twice
twin

twist
two *(the number 2)*
   [to *(toward)*]
   [too *(also)*]

ty

type
   typed
   typing
typical

ug

ugly
   uglier
   ugliest
   ugliness

ul

ultimate

um

umbrella

un

unable
uncle
undercover
underground
underline
   underlined
   underlining
underneath
understand *(irreg. vb)*
undertake
underwater
unexpected
unhappy
   unhappily
   unhappiness
uniform
   uniformity
union
unique
unit
unite
   united
   uniting

United States
unity
universe
   universal
   universality
university
   universities
unkind
unknown
unless
unlike
unload
unlucky
unnecessary
unofficial
unrest
until
unusual
unwind *(irreg. vb)*

up

up
upbeat
upbringing
upcoming
update
upend
   upended
   upending
upheaval
upholster
upon
upper
upright
uproot
upset
   upsetting
upstairs
uptown
upward

ur

uranium
urge
   urged
   urging
urgent

urn *(vase)*
   [earn *(work for)*]
Uruguay

us

us
use
   usage
   used
   using
usual

ut

Utah

va

vacant
vacation
vacuum
vague
vain *(conceited)*
   [vane *(wind indicator)*]
   [vein *(blood vessel)*]
vale *(valley)*
   [veil *(face covering)*]
vary *(change)*
   [very *(much, greatly)*]

ve

vein *(blood vessel)*
   [vain *(conceited)*]
   [vane *(wind indicator)*]
Venezuela
Venus
verb
   verbal
verbalize
   verbalized
   verbalizing
Vermont
verse
   versed
version
versus
vertical
very *(much, greatly)*
   [vary *(change)*]
vessel

The following regular endings/suffixes are not in the word list but can be added to the root word without changes: -s, -ed, -ing, -er, -est, -ly, -ful, -less, and -ness. Most exceptions and root changes are in the list.

vi

vial *(jar)*
   [vile *(bad)*]
vibrate
   vibrated
   vibrating
   vibration
vice *(bad habit)*
   [vise *(a clamp)*]
victim
victory
   victories
   victorious
view
vile *(bad)*
   [vial *(jar)*]
village
   villager
villain
vineyard
violate
   violated
   violating
   violation
violent
   violence
violet
violin
virgin
Virginia
   Virginian
vise *(clamp)*
   [vice *(bad habit)*]
visible
   visibly
vision
   visionary
visit
   visitor
vitamin

vo

vocabulary
   vocabularies
vocation
voice
   voiced
   voicing
volcano
   volcanoes

volleyball
volume
volunteer
   voluntary
vote
   voted
   voter
   voting
vowel
voyage
   voyaged
   voyager
   voyaging

wa

wade *(walk in water)*
   [weighed *(measured heaviness)*]
wage
   waged
   waging
wagon
wail *(cry)*
   [whale *(sea mammal)*]
waist *(middle of body)*
   [waste *(unused parts)*]
wait *(linger)*
   [weight *(heaviness)*]
waiter
waitress
waive *(give up rights)*
   [wave *(signal hello or good-bye)*]
wake
   waked
   waking
walk
wall
wander
want *(desire)*
   [wont *(custom)*]
war
ware *(thing for sale)*
   [wear *(have on body)*]
   [where *(what place)*]
warm
   warmth
warn
warrior
was
wash
   washes
washcloth

Washington
   Washingtonian
wasn't *(was not)*
waste *(unused parts)*
   [waist *(middle of body)*]
   wasted
   wasteful
   wasting
wastebasket
watch
   watches
watchman
water
watercolor
waterfall
waterfront
watermelon
wave *(signal hello or good-bye)*
   [waive *(give up rights)*]
   waved
   waving
wax
   waxes
way *(road)*
   [weigh *(measure heaviness)*]
   [whey *(watery part of milk)*]

we

we *(us)*
   [wee *(small)*]
weak *(not strong)*
   [week *(seven days)*]
wear *(irreg. vb)*
weather *(climate)*
   [whether *(if)*]
weatherman
weave *(interlace) (irreg. vb)*
   [we've *(we have)*]
we'd *(we would)*
   [weed *(a plant)*]
Wednesday
weed *(a plant)*
   [we'd *(we would)*]
week *(seven days)*
   [weak *(not strong)*]
weekend
weep *(irreg. vb)*
weigh *(measure heaviness)*
   [way *(road)*]
   [whey *(watery part of milk)*]
   weighed *(measured heaviness)*
   [wade *(walk in water)*]

weight (heaviness)
　[wait (linger)]
weir (dam)
　[we're (we are)]
welcome
　welcomed
　welcoming
well
we'll (we will)
　[weal (well-being)]
　[wheel (circular frame)]
went
wept
were
we're (we are)
　[weir (dam)]
weren't (were not)
west
　western
　westward
West Virginia
wet (moist) (irreg. vb)
　[whet (sharpen)]
　wetted
　wetter
　wettest
　wetting
we've (we have)
　[weave (interlace)]

wh

whale (sea mammal)
　[wail (cry)]
　whaling
what
whatever
wheat
wheel (circular frame)
　[weal (well-being)]
　[we'll (we will)]
when
whenever
where (what place)
　[ware (thing for sale)]
　[wear (have on body)]
wherever
whet (sharpen)
　[wet (moist)]

whether (if)
　[weather (climate)]
whey (watery part of milk)
　[way (road)]
　[weigh (measure heaviness)]
which (what one)
　[witch (sorceress)]
while (during)
　[wile (a trick)]
whine (complain and cry)
　[wine (a drink)]
whip
　whipped
　whipping
whirlpool
whisper
whistle
　whistled
　whistling
white
　whited
　whiten
　whiter
　whitest
whitewash
whiz
　whizzed
　whizzing
who
whoever
whole (complete)
　[hole (an opening)]
wholesale
wholly (completely)
　[holey (full of holes)]
　[holy (sacred)]
whom
whose (who owns)
　[who's (who is)]
who's (who is)
　[whose (who owns)]
why

wi

wicked
wide
　widen
　wider
　widest

width
wife
　wives
wild
wildcat
wilderness
wile (a trick)
　[while (during)]
will
win
　winner
　winning
wind (irreg. vb)
windmill
window
windpipe
windshield
wine (a drink)
　[whine (cry and complain)]
wing
　winged
　winging
　wingless
wink
winter
wipe
　wiped
　wiper
　wiping
wire
　wired
　wiring
wiretapping
Wisconsin
wise
　wiser
　wisest
wish
　wishes
wit
witch (sorceress)
　[which (what one)]
　witches
with
withdraw
　withdrawal
　withdrawn

The following regular endings/suffixes are not in the word list but can be added to the root word without changes: -s, -ed, -ing, -er, -est, -ly, -ful, -less, and -ness. Most exceptions and root changes are in the list.

withhold
within
without
withstand
witness
wittingly
witty
  wittier
  wittiest
  wittily
  wittiness
wizard
  wizardry

wo

wobble
  wobbled
  wobbling
woe
woebegone
woke
wolf
  wolfish
  wolves
woman *(one female)*
  [women *(several females)*]
won *(triumphed)*
  [one *(the number 1)*]
wonder
  wondrous
wonderland
wont *(custom)*
  [want *(desire)*]
  won't *(would not)*
wood *(of a tree)*
  [would *(is willing to)*]
woodchuck
woodland
woodpecker
woodpile
woodshed
woodsy
woodwork
wool
  woolen
  woolier
  wooliest
word
  wordier
  wordiest
  wordy
wore

work
  workable
workshop
world
  worldlier
  worldliest
  worldliness
  worldly
worm
worn
worry
  worried
  worrier
worse
  worsen
worship
  worshipped
  worshipper
  worshipping
worst *(most bad)*
  [wurst *(sausage)*]
worth
worthy
worthwhile
would *(is willing to)*
  [wood *(of a tree)*]
wouldn't *(would not)*
wound
wove
  woven

wr

wrap *(cover)*
  [rap *(hit)*]
  wrapped
  wrapping
wreak *(inflict)*
  [reek *(give off strong odor)*]
wreck
wrench
  wrenches
wrest *(take from)*
  [rest *(relax)*]
wring *(squeeze) (irreg. vb)*
  [ring *(circular band)*]
wristwatch
write *(inscribe) (irreg. vb)*
  [right *(correct)*]
  [rite *(ceremony)*]
  writer
  writing
  written

wrong
wrote *(did write)*
  [rote *(by memory)*]
wrung *(squeezed)*
  [rung *(step on a ladder)*]
wry *(ironically humorous)*
  [rye *(grain)*]

wu

wurst *(sausage)*
  [worst *(most bad)*]

wy

Wyoming

x

x-ray

xy

xylophone

ya

yacht
yard
yarn

ye

year
yell
yellow
  yellowish
yelp
yes
  yeses
yesterday
yesteryear
yet
yew *(a shrub)*
  [ewe *(female sheep)*]
  [you *(yourself)*]

yo

yoke *(harness)*
  [yolk *(egg center)*]
you *(yourself)*
  [ewe *(female sheep)*]
  [yew *(a shrub)*]
you'd *(you would)*

you'll *(you will)*
    [yule *(Christmas)*]
you're *(you are)*
    [your *(belonging to you)*]
you've *(you have)*
young
    younger
    youngest
your *(belonging to you)*
    [you're *(you are)*]
yours
yourself
youth

yu

Yugoslavia
yule *(Christmas)*
    [you'll *(you will)*]

ze

zeal
    zealous
zebra
zero
    zeroed
    zeroes
    zeroing
zest
zestful

zi

zip
    zipped
    zipping
zipper

zo

zone
    zoned
    zoning
zoo
    zookeeper
    zoology

The following regular endings/suffixes are not in the word list but can be added to the root word without changes: -s, -ed, -ing, -er, -est, -ly, -ful, -less, and -ness. Most exceptions and root changes are in the list.

SPELLING RULES

PLURALS AND *S* FORM OF VERBS

(The more important rules have bold-faced type.)

a. Add -*s* to most nouns and verbs: *cows, runs* (*Note:* Adding -*s* does not add a syllable to the root word.)
b. Add -*es* if the word ends in *ch, sh, x, s,* or *z: box—boxes; approach—approaches* (*Note:* Adding -*es* adds a syllable to the root word.)

For words ending in *y*

c. If the word ends in a *y* preceded by a consonant, change the *y* to *i* and add -*es*: *baby—babies; cry—cries*
d. *Note:* Don't change *y* if a vowel precedes it: *key—keys*
e. Also don't change *y* if the word is a proper noun: one *Kathy*—two *Kathys*

For words ending in *o*

f. For a few words ending in *o*, add -*es*: *go—goes*
g. However, for many words ending in *o*, just adding an -*s* is OK because either spelling is correct: *banjos* or *banjoes*
h. If the *o* is preceded by a vowel, just add -*s*: *radio—radios*

For words ending in *f*

i. For a few nouns ending in *f* (or *fe*), change the *f* to *v* and add -*es*: *leaf—leaves; wife—wives*

Other Plurals

j. Some foreign nouns have different plurals: *alumnus—alumni; index—indices*
k. A few nouns in English have different plurals: *foot—feet*
l. A few nouns don't change for plurals: one *deer*—two *deer*
m. Symbols form plurals with an apostrophe: Mind your *p*'s and *q*'s.

ADDING ENDINGS AND SUFFIXES

A *word ending* or *suffix* is a word part that is added to the end of a root word.

Basic Rule: Just add the ending or suffix to the root word.
Regular examples: *want—wanted, wanting, wants* (Important: See plurals list above.)
Exceptions:
For words ending in e

a. Drop the final *e* if the ending or suffix begins with a vowel: *rose—rosy; name—naming, named*
b. Keep the final *e* if the suffix begins with a consonant: *safe—safely*
c. Keep the final *e* if a vowel precedes it: *see—seeing*
d. Drop the final *le* if the suffix is -*ly* (no double *l*): *able—ably*

For words ending in *y*

e. Change the *y* to *i* if *y* is preceded by a consonant: *carry—carried* (Ending here is -*ed*.)
f. Don't change the *y* to *i* if *y* is preceded by a vowel: *joy—joyful*
g. Don't change the *y* to *i* if the ending begins with an *i*: *carry—carrying* (Ending here is -*ing*.)

For words ending in *c*

   h. Add a *k* before any ending or suffix beginning with an *e*, *i*, or *y*: *picnic—picnicking;*
      panic—panicky

Doubling the final letter

   i. **Double the final consonant before adding the ending or suffix if all of these**
      conditions are true:

       1. the word has one syllable (or the final syllable is accented)
       2. the word ends in a single consonant (other than *x***)**
       3. the word has a single vowel letter
       4. the ending or suffix begins with a vowel
      Examples: *brag—bragged;* **the** *x* **exception:** *box—boxing*

   j. Do not double the final consonant (Basic Rule applies) if:

       1. the suffix begins with a consonant: *equip—equipment*
       2. the vowel sound has two letters: *rain—rained*
       3. the word has two final consonants: *hard—harder*
       4. the final syllable is not accented: *benefit—benefited*

   k. If the word has two syllables and is accented on the last syllable, treat it as a one-
      syllable word (See i. and j. above): *admit—admittance*

   l. If the word has two syllables and is accented on the first syllable, do not double the
      last letter (back to Basic Rule): *equal—equaled*

   m.The final *l* is kept when adding *-ly* (this really restates i. and j., but it looks strange to
      see two *l*'s): *cool—coolly*

ADDING PREFIXES

A *prefix* is a word part that is added to the beginning of a root word.

Basic Rule: Prefixes never change spelling. They are just added to whole words.

   a. Adding a prefix sometimes results in double letters: *misspell, illegible*
   b. Often the prefixes *ex-* and *self-* use a hyphen: *ex-resident, self-help*

ei or *ie* RULE

Basic Rule: Write *i* before *e*, except after *c*.

    Example: *chief, believe*

   a. If the vowel sounds like long *a*, spell it *ei*: *neighbor, weigh*
   b. **There are plenty of exceptions:** *their, Neil, science, either, leisure*

COMPOUND WORDS

**Basic Rule: Keep the full spelling of both words. Just join them together without
a hyphen.**

    Example: *ear + ring = earring; room + mate = roommate*

A more common usage or more specific meaning tends to make two words into a
compound word: *blackbird* (one word), as opposed to *black car*, which are two words.

SPELLING USING PHONICS

Many people think phonics rules are useful in learning to read, and they are. But phonics is also important in learning to spell because the sound/letter (phoneme-grapheme) correspondence works both ways. It is unfortunate that there are so many exceptions or variations on sound/letter correspondence (phonics isn't perfect), but there are still plenty of words and parts of words with regular spellings. Look over the following two charts for vowels and consonants. If you know that much phonics, you will be able to spell many words and parts of words correctly.

You might say that the letter/sound correspondences in these two charts are a set of spelling rules based on phonics. Young children use invented spelling, which is really a kind of partial knowledge of phonics. As children get older, or as writers mature, they still use invented spelling sometimes. Their made-up spelling has improved, however, because they know more phonics and because they have learned the spelling of many letter clusters.

The following charts can also help you look up words in the Spelling Checker word list. If you can sound out words (know the phonemes), you can look up their common and less common spellings in the charts.

All vowels and some consonants can be spelled in more than one way. Three consonant letters, *c, q,* and *x*, have no sound (phoneme) of their own. The letter *c* can represent either a /k/ or an /s/ sound. The letter *c* generally represents the /s/ sound before *i, e,* and *y*, and it represents the /k/ sound before *a, o,* and *u*. The letter *q* always appears with a *u*, and *qu* represents the /kw/ sound. The letter *x* usually represents the /ks/ sound.

The letter *g* can be sounded like a /g/ or a /j/. The letter *s* can represent a /z/ or an /s/ sound, but it represents the /z/ sound only at the end of certain words. A **digraph** refers to two letters that represent a sound. The digraph *th* has two sounds: voiced as in *them* and unvoiced as in *thin*.

The letter *y* is a consonant at the beginning of most words and a vowel in the middle or end of a word. See Vowel Exceptions in the chart on page 71.

Most linguists and dictionaries say that the digraph *wh* really represents the /hw/ blend, but this is a highly technical point lost on most spellers and speakers of English. The same is true for the digraph *ng* that is a unique phoneme /ng/.

The **schwa sound** is the unaccented vowel sound that sounds much like a short /u/. It is helpful to remember that to have an unaccented vowel the word must also have at least one other accented vowel sound.

In a **blend,** two different phonemes (sounds) occur together so that both are sounded; for example, the *bl* in *black*. This is different from a consonant digraph like *sh*, which makes its own phoneme. It is not a blend of /s/ and /h/. The digraphs are in the charts.

Last but not least, it is important to remember that there are plenty of exceptions to the phonics presented in the vowel and consonant charts. That is why you have to learn to spell many words by "sight," or the whole word approach. It is also why the Spelling Checker word list should be your constant companion when writing anything.

VOWEL SOUNDS (alphabetical order)

Phoneme		Common Spelling	Less Common Spelling
short /a/	/ă/	**a** hat	
long /a/	/ā/	**a–e** age, **ai** aid	**eigh** eight, **ay** say, **ey** prey
broad /a/	/ä/	**a (r)** far	**a** father
short /e/	/ĕ/	**e** red	**ea** head
long /e/	/ē/	**e** repay, **ee** see	**ea** seat, **y** lazy
short /i/	/ĭ/	**i** bit	**y** gym
long /i/	/ī/	**i–e** ice, **y** try, **i** child	**ie** pie
short /o/	/ŏ/	**o** hot	**a** watch
long /o/	/ō/	**o** so, **o–e** nose	**oa** boat, **ow** know
broad /o/	/ô/	**o (r)** for, **o** loss **a (w)** awful	**a (l)** all, **a (u)** auto
/oi/, /oy/	/oi/	**oi** boil, **oy** boy	
/ou/, /ow/	/ou/	**ou** out, **ow** owl	
long /oo/	/o͞o/	**oo** moon	**u** ruby, **ew** chew, **o** do, **ou** soup, **u–e** duke
short /oo/	/o͝o/	**oo** good	**u (l)** pull, **ou** could
short /u/	/ŭ/	**u** nut	**o** son
long /u/	/ū/	**u–e** use, **u** music	
∂ Schwa	/∂/	**a** alone, **e** taken, **i** direct, **il** pencil, **ou** generous, **o** riot, **u** campus	

(Some dictionaries say that the schwa phoneme is the unaccented vowel sound, so it must appear in a polysyllable word. Others say that schwa and short /u/ are the same.)

VOWEL SOUNDS (clustered)

Short Vowels

a-at	/ă/
e-end	/ĕ/
i-is	/ĭ/
o-hot	/ŏ/
u-up	/ŭ/

Long Vowels Open Syllable Rule

a-baby	/ā/
e-we	/ē/
i-idea	/ī/
o-so	/ō/

Long Vowels Final *e* Rule

a-make	/ā/
e-eve	/ē/
i-five	/ī/
o-home	/ō/
u-use	/ū/

Long Vowel Digraphs

ai-aid	/ā/
ay-say	/ā/
ea-eat	/ē/
ee-see	/ē/
oa-oat	/ō/
ow-own	/ō/

Schwa

a-comma	/ə/
e-happen	/ə/
o-atom	/ə/

Vowel *y*

y-try	/ī/
y-funny	/ē/

Vowel Plus *r*

er-her	/ur/
ir-sir	/ur/
ur-fur	/ur/
ar-far	/är/
or-for	/ôr/

Diphthongs

oi-oil	/oi/
oy-boy	/oi/
ou-out	/ou/
ow-how	/ou/

Double /o/

oo-soon	/o͞o/
oo-good	/o͝o/
u-truth	/o͞o/
u-put	/o͝o/

Broad /o/

o-song	/ô/
a (l)-also	/ô/
a (w)-saw	/ô/
a (u)-auto	/ô/

Vowel Exceptions

ea-bread	/ĕ/	In a few words, *ea* stands for the short /e/ sound.
e (silent)-come		In a few words, final *e* does **not** indicate that the preceding vowel is long.
y-yes	/y/	*y* is a consonant at the beginning of a word.
le-candle	/əl/	final *le* represents the sound of schwa plus /l/.
al-pedal	/əl/	final *al* represents the sound of schwa plus /l/.
il-pencil	/əl/	final *il* represents the sound of schwa plus /l/.
ul-awful	/əl/	final *ul* represents the sound of schwa plus /l/.

CONSONANT SOUNDS (alphabetical order)

Phoneme	Common Spelling	Less Common Spelling
/b/	**b** boy	
[c]	(no *c* phoneme; see /k/ and /s/)	
/ch/	**ch** cheese	**t** nature
/d/	**d** dog	
/f/	**f** fat	**ph** phone, **gh** laugh
/g/	**g** girl	
/gz/	**x** exert	
/h/	**h** hot	
/j/	**j** just, **g** giant	
/k/	**c** cat, **k** king	**ck** sick, **ch** chrome
/ks/	**x** fox (no *x* phoneme)	
/kw/	**qu** quick (no *q* phoneme)	
/l/	**l** look	
/m/	**m** me	
/n/	**n** no	**kn** knife
/ng/	**ng** sing	
/p/	**p** put	
[q]	(no *q* phoneme; see /kw/)	
/r/	**r** run	**wr** write
/s/	**s** sit, **c** city	
/sh/	**sh** shut, **ti** action	**s** sugar, **ch** chute
/t/	**t** toy	
/th/ (voiced)	**th** this	
/th/ (voiceless)	**th** thing	
/v/	**v** voice	
/w/	**w** will	
/wh/	**wh** white	
[x]	(no *x* phoneme; see /ks/ and /gz/)	
/y/ (consonant)	**y** you	**i** onion
/z/	**s** his, **z** zero	
/zh/	**si** vision	**su** pleasure, **ge** beige

CONSONANT SOUNDS (clustered)

Single Consonants That Usually Stand for Specific Single Sounds

b	j	p	w
d	k	r	y
f	l	s	z
g	m	t	
h	n	v	

Consonant Digraphs That Usually Stand for Specific Single Sounds

ch as in *church*
sh as in *shoe*
th (voiced) as in *this*
th (voiceless) as in *thin*
wh (*hw* blend) as in *which*

Other Important Spelling-Sound Connections

c = /k/ before *a*, *o*, or *u* as in *car*
c = /s/ before *i*, *e*, or *y*, as in *city*
ch = /k/ as in *character*
ch = /sh/ as in *chef*
g = /j/ before *i*, *e*, or *y*, as in *gem*
ge = /zh/ as in *massage*
gh = /f/ as in *laugh*
i = /y/ as in *million*
ng = /ng/ unique phoneme, as in *sing*
ph = /f/ as in *phone*

qu = /kw/ blend as in *quick*
   (the letter *q* is never used
   without *u*)
s = /z/ as in *has*
s = /sh/ as in *sure*
si = /zh/ as in *vision*
su = /zh/ as in *measure*
t = /ch/ as in *capture*
ti = /sh/ as in *attention*
x = /ks/ blend, as in *fox*
x = /gz/ blend, as in *exact*

Common Beginning Consonant Blends

br	bl	sc	scr	dw
cr	cl	sk	squ	tw
dr	fl	sm	str	
fr	gl	sn	spr	
gr	pl	sp	spl	
pr	sl	st	shr	
tr		sw	sch	
wr			thr	

Silent Consonants

gn = /n/ as in *gnat*
kn = /n/ as in *knife*
wr = /r/ as in *write*
igh = /i/ as in *right*
ck = /k/ as in *back*
mb = /m/ as in *lamb*
lf = /f/ as in *calf*
lk = /k/ as in *walk*
tle = /əl/ as in *castle*

Common Final Consonant Blends

ct-*act*	**lt**-*salt*	**nk**-*ink*	**rd**-*hard*	**sk**-*risk*
ft-*lift*	**mp**-*jump*	**nt**-*ant*	**rk**-*dark*	**sp**-*lisp*
ld-*old*	**nd**-*and*	**pt**-*kept*	**rt**-*art*	**st**-*least*

CAPITALIZATION

A. **Capitalize all proper nouns.**

1. **Names**
   Example: Abraham Lincoln

2. **Specific titles**
   Example: When President Abraham Lincoln spoke, the people cheered.

3. **Countries, states, geographic areas**
   Examples: France, Missouri, the East, the Sierras, Lake Erie, the Colorado (River)

4. **Streets, roads, avenues**
   Examples: Hill St., First Avenue

5. **Religious names and all pronouns relating to the deity**
   Examples: God, Jesus Christ, Mohammed, His, Thine, Bible, Catholic, Jewish

6. **Days, months**
   Examples: Thursday, April

7. **Schools, buildings**
   Examples: Elmore Community College, University of Southern California, Empire State Building

8. **Holidays**
   Examples: Christmas, Memorial Day, Fourth of July

9. **Racial and cultural groups**
   Examples: African American, Asian, Hispanic, Indian, Native American

10. **Trade names, companies, organizations**
    Examples: Nabisco, General Foods Corporation, American Heart Association

B. **Capitalize the first word in a sentence.**
   Example: The men don't want to go to war.

C. **Capitalize the first word in each line of most poetry.**
   Example: "... If I were a dead leaf thou mightest bear,
               If I were a swift cloud to fly with thee;
               A wave to pant beneath thy power, and share ... "
                        —from "Ode to the West Wind," by Percy Bysshe Shelley

D. **Capitalize all main words in a title.**
Example: The new book is *Making a Difference in the World.*

E. **Capitalize the first word in a quote.**
Example: He said, "If I can't have it, nobody will."

Do not capitalize the following:

1. **Prepositions, articles, or conjunctions in a title unless these words have more than four letters.** But always capitalize verbs, no matter how small, and *to* as part of the infinitive verb form.
Example: We heard an interesting speech, "Communication Is About Listening: How To Choose the Right Time."

2. **Seasons**
Example: The frost was a sign that winter was near.

3. **Directions of the compass**
Example: Our friend's house was west of town.

4. **Words in quotations if only part of the quotation is used**
Example: The dean had "mixed feelings" about the new school legislation.

5. **A word that is a general, not a specific, description of a person or thing.** Note the title *president* and the word *college* in the following example: *The class president was the first one at the college graduation.* But specific persons and titles are capitalized in the following example: *Even President Clinton attended the Kansas City College Commencement.*

PUNCTUATION

Period

1. At the end of a sentence: *Birds fly.*
2. After some abbreviations: *Mr., U.S.A.*
3. In decimal fractions: *5.05, 3.15*

Question Mark

1. At the end of a question: *Who is he?*
2. To express doubt: *He weighs 250 (?) pounds.*

Apostrophe

1. To show possession: *Bill's daughter*
2. Omitted letter, letters, or numbers: *isn't, '93*
3. To avoid confusion in forming certain plurals: *Dot your* i*'s, and cross your* t*'s.*

Parentheses

1. Supplementary material: *The map (see illustration) is good.*
2. Stronger than commas: *Joe (the bad guy) is dead.*
3. Enclose numbers: *Her car is (1) a Ford and (2) too slow.*

Colon

1. Introduce a series: *She has three things: money, brains, and charm.*
2. Separate subtitles: *The Book: How To Read It*
3. Set off a clause: *He's not heavy: he's my brother.*
4. Business letter salutation: *Dear Sir:*
5. Times and ratios: *7:45 A.M.; mix it 3:1*

Semicolon

1. Stronger than a comma: *Peace is difficult; war is hell.*
2. Separate clauses containing commas: *He was tired; therefore, he quit.*

Quotation Marks

1. Speech as dialogue: *She said, "Hello."*
2. Titles of songs and short stories: *He read "The Gift of the Magi."*
3. Special words or slang: *He is "nuts."*
4. Direct quote: *He told me that he "never lied."*

Comma

1. Independent clauses: *I like him, and he is tall.*
2. Dependent clause that precedes a main clause: *After the game, we went home.*
3. Semi-parenthetical phrase or clause: *Bill, the tall one, is here.*
4. Series: *He likes clothes, movies, and sports.*
5. Multiple adjectives: *The big, bad, ugly wolf howled.*
6. In dialogue: *She said, "Hello."*
7. Dates: *July 4, 1776*
8. Titles: *Joe Smith, Ph.D.*
9. Informal letter salutation: *Dear Danita,*
10. Letter closing: *Yours truly,*
11. Inverted names: *Smith, Joe*
12. Separate city and state: *Los Angeles, California*
13. In numerals: *43,126*

Exclamation Point

1. To show strong emotion: *She is the best!*
2. After interjections: *Help!*

Hyphen

1. To separate parts of some compound words: *son-in-law; self-respect*
2. To separate the two-number words used to name amounts from 21–29, 31–39, and so on, up to 99: *twenty-one, ninety-nine.*
3. To show duration: *1949–50; Rome–London*

Dash

1. To show sudden change in thought: *I stopped suddenly—I'm not sure why—and ran in the opposite direction.*
2. To show word omissions: *She called him a —.*

Ellipsis

1. To show omitted material: *He . . . went home.*

THE APOSTROPHE

A. Use an apostrophe to show possession.

1. For a singular possessive not ending in *s*, add an apostrophe and *s*.
    Example: *The <u>student's</u> book is lost.*

2. For a possessive of a plural ending in *s*, add only an apostrophe after the *s*.
    Example: *There were many <u>students'</u> books lost.*

3. For a possessive of the singular form of a word that ends in *s*, add an apostrophe and the *s*.
    Example: *Mrs. <u>Cross's</u> car*

4. To show joint possession, add an apostrophe to the last of the names listed.
    Example: *John and Nancy: John and Nancy<u>'s</u> house*

5. In compound words, add an apostrophe to the last part of the compound.
    Examples: *sister-in-law: sister-in-law<u>'s</u>; No one else: no one else<u>'s</u>*

B. Use an apostrophe to show omission.

To show the omission of letters, such as in contractions, or numbers, such as in years, add an apostrophe.
Examples: *cannot: can<u>'t</u>*
            of the clock: <u>o'</u>clock
            1989 Chevy: <u>'</u>89 Chevy

C. Use an apostrophe with *s* to show the plural of letters when omitting the apostrophe would lead to confusion.

Examples: *You use too many* I*'s when you speak.*
            Mind your p*'s and* q*'s.*

WHEN NOT TO USE AN APOSTROPHE

Many writers overuse the apostrophe. Too often, they add one at the end of words ending in *s*.

Do not use an apostrophe:

1. To indicate the simple plural
   Correct: *The McKees are coming over tonight.*

              The two cats are both white.

2. With pronouns such as *its, hers, ours,* and *whose*
   Correct: *The purse is hers.*

Note regarding *its* and *it's*: Use an apostrophe only to indicate the contraction for *it is* or *it has*:

   Example: *It's been a stressful day.*

              The barn lost its roof.

ABBREVIATIONS

U.S. Post Office Authorized State Abbreviations
(Note: No periods)

U.S. Territory Abbreviations

Alabama	AL
Alaska	AK
American Samoa	AS
Arizona	AZ
Arkansas	AR
California	CA
Canal Zone	CZ
Colorado	CO
Connecticut	CT
Delaware	DE
District of Columbia	DC
Florida	FL
Georgia	GA
Guam	GU
Hawaii	HI
Idaho	ID
Illinois	IL
Indiana	IN
Iowa	IA
Kansas	KS
Kentucky	KY
Louisiana	LA
Maine	ME
Maryland	MD
Massachusetts	MA
Michigan	MI
Minnesota	MN
Mississippi	MS
Missouri	MO
Montana	MT
Nebraska	NE
Nevada	NV
New Hampshire	NH
New Jersey	NJ
New Mexico	NM
New York	NY
North Carolina	NC
North Dakota	ND
Ohio	OH
Oklahoma	OK
Oregon	OR
Pennsylvania	PA
Puerto Rico	PR
Rhode Island	RI
South Carolina	SC
South Dakota	SD
Tennessee	TN
Texas	TX
Utah	UT
Vermont	VT
Virginia	VA
Virgin Islands	VI
Washington	WA
West Virginia	WV
Wisconsin	WI
Wyoming	WY

Also approved for use in addressing mail are the following street abbreviations:

Alley	Aly
Boulevard	Blvd
Branch	Br
Bypass	Byp
Causeway	Cswy
Center	Ctr
Circle	Cir
Court	Ct
Courts	Cts
Crescent	Cres
Drive	Dr
Expressway	Expy
Extension	Ext
Freeway	Fwy
Gardens	Gdns
Grove	Grv
Heights	Hts
Highway	Hwy
Lane	Ln
Place	Pl
Plaza	Plz
Point	Pt
Road	Rd
Rural	R
Square	Sq
Street	St
Terrace	Ter
Trail	Trl
Turnpike	Tpke
Vista	Vis

Titles

Mister. . . . . Mr.
Married woman . . . . Mrs.
Unmarried woman . . . . Miss
Any woman . . . . Ms.
Doctor . . . . Dr.
Reverend . . . . Rev.
Father. . . . . Fr.
Senator. . . . . Sen.
Representative . . . . Rep.
Honorable (judge). . . . . Hon.
Governor . . . . Gov.
President . . . . Pres.
Vice President . . . . V.P.

Time

Before noon. . . . . A.M.
(ante meridian)
After noon . . . . P.M.
(post meridian)
Eastern Standard Time . . . . EST
Eastern Daylight Time . . . . EDT
Central Standard Time . . . . CST
Central Daylight Time . . . . CDT
Mountain Standard Time . . . . MST
Mountain Daylight Time . . . . MDT
Pacific Standard Time. . . . . PST
Pacific Daylight Time . . . . PDT
Greenwich Mean Time . . . . GMT
Minute. . . . . min.
Second . . . . sec.

Scholarly Degrees and Titles of Respect

Bachelor of Arts. . . . . B.A.
Bachelor of Science . . . . B.S.
Doctor of Dental Surgery . . . . D.D.S.
Master of Arts . . . . M.A.
Doctor of Medicine. . . . . M.D.
Doctor of Philosophy . . . . Ph.D.
Bachelor of Laws . . . . L.L.B.
Certified Public Accountant . . . . . . C.P.A.

Months

January. . . . . Jan.
February . . . . Feb.
March. . . . . Mar.
April. . . . . Apr.
May . . . . May
June . . . . June
July. . . . . July
August . . . . Aug.
September . . . . Sept.
October . . . . Oct.
November . . . . Nov.
December. . . . . Dec.

Days of the Week

Sunday. . . . . Sun.
Monday . . . . Mon.
Tuesday . . . . Tues.
Wednesday. . . . . Wed.
Thursday . . . . Thurs.
Friday. . . . . Fri.
Saturday. Sat.

Parts of Speech

adjective . . . . adj.

adverb . . . . adv.

conjunction . . . . conj.

interjection . . . . inter.

noun . . . . n.

preposition . . . . prep.

pronoun . . . . pron.

verb . . . . vb.

(For explanations of Parts of Speech, see page 93.)

Reference Abbreviations Commonly Used

cont. . . . . continued

etc. (Latin) . . . . *et cetera*, and so forth
    (in speech, *etc.* is pronounced et-SET-uh-ruh)

i.e. (Latin) . . . . *id est*, that is

misc. . . . . miscellaneous

p. . . . . page

pp. . . . . pages

PS (Latin) . . . . *postscriptum*, postscript

PPS . . . . *post postscriptum*, a later postscript

vol. . . . . volume

ex. or Ex. . . . . example

CONTRACTIONS

Contractions are combinations of two words to make a shorter word.

am
I'm

is, has
he's
she's
it's
what's

would, had
I'd
you'd
he'd
she'd
we'd
they'd
it'd
there'd
what'd
who'd

not
can't
don't
isn't
won't
shouldn't
couldn't
wouldn't
aren't
doesn't
wasn't
weren't
hasn't
haven't
hadn't

are
you're
we're
they're
who're

us
let's

have
I've
you've
we've
they've
could've
would've
should've
might've
who've
there've

will
I'll
you'll
she'll
he'll
it'll
we'll
they'll
that'll
these'll
those'll
there'll
this'll
what'll
who'll

GRAMMAR

SENTENCES: BASIC CONSTRUCTION

Part of grammar (rules on language use) is about different types of sentences. The study of patterns used in sentences is also called **syntax.** Here is a simplified explanation of some common sentence types:

Minimum sentence

The basic rule is that every sentence must have a noun (or pronoun) and a verb. The noun (or pronoun) is called the **simple subject** of the sentence. The verb is the most important word in the **predicate** of the sentence. A predicate of a sentence is the main action happening to it. Sometimes the verb is the only word in the predicate. Thus the minimum sentence looks like this: *Birds sing.*

	Birds	*sing.*
USAGE IN SENTENCE:	simple subject +	predicate
PART OF SPEECH:	noun +	verb

Typical sentence

Most sentences have more than two words. Words that modify the simple subject are in the **complete subject.** All other words are part of the **complete predicate.** The verb itself is called either the **simple predicate** or the **verb.**

	The little red birds	*sing sweetly in the morning.*
USAGE IN SENTENCE:	complete subject +	complete predicate
PART OF SPEECH:	modifiers + noun +	verb + modifiers

Sentence with object

Some sentences are incomplete without an object. The **object** receives the action of the verb.

	Birds	*build*	*nests.*
USAGE IN SENTENCE:	simple subject +	verb +	object
PART OF SPEECH:	noun +	verb +	noun

Modifying the subject

Each part of a sentence can be modified by adding another word or words. Here, the subject is modified: *The big red birds build nests.*

	The	*big*	*red*	*birds*	*build*	*nests.*
USAGE IN SENTENCE:	modifiers	+		s. subject +	verb +	object
PART OF SPEECH:	article +	adjective +	adjective +	noun +	verb +	noun

Modifying the predicate

	Birds	*quickly build*	*nests.*
USAGE IN SENTENCE:	s. subject +	modifier + verb +	object
PART OF SPEECH:	noun +	adverb + verb +	noun

Modifying the object

	Birds	build	safe nests.
USAGE IN SENTENCE:	s. subject + verb +	modifier + object	
PART OF SPEECH:	noun + verb +	adjective + noun	

All of these ideas can appear in the same sentence:

	The big red	birds	quickly	build	safe	nests.
USAGE IN SENTENCE:	modifiers +	s. subject +	modifier +	verb +	modifier +	object
PART OF SPEECH:	article + adj. + adj. +	noun +	adv. +	verb +	adj. +	noun

Prepositional phrases

A **prepositional phrase** is a combination of two or more words that begin with a preposition and that does not contain both a subject and a verb. A prepositional phrase can be added to a sentence in several places. The following sentences illustrate how the prepositional phrase *at night* can be placed in different parts of a sentence:

> *Birds fly home at night.*
> *At night, birds fly home.*
> *Birds, at night, fly home.*

The first sentence is probably the best sentence because it flows better than the others. The second sentence is a bit awkward, but maybe the writer wants to stress the night part of the message. The third sentence may be grammatically correct, but it is awkward because the placement of *at night* puts distance between the subject (*birds*) and the verb (*fly*).

Clauses

A **clause** is a group of words containing a subject (noun or pronoun) and a verb that can be added to a sentence.

> *He took a bath <u>before he ate dinner</u>.*

The words *before he ate dinner* form a **dependent clause.** This clause can't stand alone the way a sentence can because the word *before* creates a condition that must be satisfied. The words *He took a bath* form an **independent clause.** It could stand alone if the writer wanted to shorten the sentence.

Negative sentence

You can also make a sentence such as *Birds sing* mean the opposite (or negative) by adding a word or two like *no* or *not*.

> *No birds sing.*
> *Birds do not sing.*

Questions

One way to make a sentence into a question is to put the verb in front of the subject.

> *Are they lost?*

Questions also frequently begin with one of the *Wh*-questions—*Who, What, Why, When, Where, Which* (or *How*).

> *Which birds fly?*

Another way to make a question is to split the verb and its helping verb and put the helping verb before the subject.

Can birds fly?	*Can*	*birds*	*fly?*
	(helping verb)	(subject)	(verb)

Sentence combining

Sometimes sentences can be improved by combining two short sentences into one longer sentence.

> *Men go to work. + Women go to work.*
> *Men and women go to work.*

Sentence untangling

Sometimes sentences get hopelessly long or tangled up. Although technically they are correct sentences, you can make them more understandable by dividing them into two or more sentences.

> *After losing almost all the games during the season, the school that the boys went to won the big basketball game last year.*

> Better: *The boys' school won the big basketball game last year. It lost most of the other games during the season.*

Student writers sometimes make awkward sentences by using *and* too often. These are called **run-on sentences.** Breaking a clumsy sentence into two or more sentences often improves the flow of the writing.

> *I went home and I greeted my dog and I gave him something to eat and I played with him.*

> Correct: *When I went home I greeted my dog. I gave him something to eat and played with him.*

SENTENCES: ADVANCED CONSTRUCTION

1. Vary sentence length.
Good writers use a combination of long and short sentences.

> *Short sentences have punch. Long, involved sentences sometimes are necessary, but they are often harder to read and leave the reader confused.*

2. Vary word order.
The typical sentence is called a **declarative sentence,** and it uses the order subject-verb-object. Example: *Birds fly home after dark.*

You can add variety by starting with a verb phrase.

> *Flying home after dark is what some birds like.*
> *To fly home is important for some birds.*

3. Use the active voice.
The active voice is livelier, easier to read, and uses fewer words.

> *Miguel read the book.* (active voice)
> *The book was read by Miguel.* (passive voice)
> *Rattlesnakes should not be stepped on.* (passive voice)
> *Don't step on rattlesnakes.* (active voice)

There are times when you want to use the passive voice in order to emphasize something. For example, if in discussing a canceled football game, you wish to emphasize the football game instead of its cancelation, you might use the following passive sentence:

> *The football game was canceled because of rain.*

4. Avoid negative sentences.
It is better to state things positively. Watch out for the word *not.*

> *Carla did not tell the truth.* (negative)
> *Carla told a lie.* (positive)

5. Be specific.
Use specific examples and descriptions. Something **specific,** or **concrete,** is something you can see, feel, hear, or touch.

> *The crowd was noisy.* (abstract)
> *The crowd was yelling and screaming.* (specific)
> *He was a big man.* (abstract)
> *He was nearly seven feet tall.* (specific)

BUILD A SENTENCE

Select a word or phrase from each column.

Who?	Did What?	Why?	When?	Where?
A boy	climbed into an airplane	for a vacation	last summer	in New York
				on the moon
The shark	looked everywhere	to find his mother	in 2020	outside my house
A big truck	slid	to get a million dollars	during the game	in a cave
				on a farm
The monster	laughed	for fun	next year	under a rock
My son	swam			
	dove	because he/she was on fire	at midnight	next to a lion
A rattlesnake	swung on a rope		forever	100 feet beneath the ocean
Maria	fell	to fall in love		
The quarterback		for an ice cream cone	before breakfast	in bed
A tiny ant	yelled loudly		always	on top of a tree
	flew	to build a house		at the circus
The train	ran fast		500 years ago	in front of the city hall
		to fight the enemy	right now	in a cornfield
The detective	jumped		in a month	behind the stove
A beautiful actress	kicked	to get to class	after work	in space
	couldn't stop	to be kissed		
A large bird	slithered		in an hour	inside an egg
		for a coat of paint	yesterday	in Africa
My good friend	crawled			out West
			during the war	on a tropical island
A teacher	hopped on one foot	because it was angry	at dawn	

Feel free to add more words to make your sentence read better or add interest. You can leave out anything except a subject and a verb.

VERB ERRORS

As a writer, you must pay particular attention to the correct use of verbs to be sure your meaning is clear to readers. Recall the meaning of *subject* and *verb*. The **subject** of a sentence answers the question *who?* or *what?* The **predicate** of a sentence is the main action happening in it. The most important part of the predicate is the **verb.** In this sentence, *Gina rides the bus every morning*, the subject is *Gina* and the verb is *rides*.

Because it needs to be correct and exact, written English follows more formal rules than spoken English. Sometimes when you speak in casual situations, you may choose to ignore some grammar rules. However, when you write and when you revise, you need to keep the rules in mind. Be sure to avoid the following common errors in verb usage.

Error Number 1: Lack of Agreement Between Subject and Verb (Person and Number)

A verb must agree with its subject in **number**. Reread the sentence above. *Gina* is the name of only one person, so the verb the writer uses—*rides*—is one that agrees with a singular subject. Now read this sentence: *Many workers ride the bus every morning*. In this sentence, the subject, *Many workers*, names more than one person. So the verb that is used—*ride*—is one that agrees with a plural subject.

Refer to the chart at the bottom of the page to see how a regular verb changes according to the number of the subject.

A verb must also agree with its subject in **person**. In English, there are three categories that explain the relationship of a person to the speaker. The categories are first, second, and third person. The first person refers to the speaker himself or herself. Subjects in the first person use the words *I* and *we*.

Example: *I ride* the downtown bus.

The second person refers to the person the speaker is addressing. Subjects in the second person use the word *you*.

Example: *You* ride the downtown bus.

The third person refers to the person the speaker is talking about. Subjects in the third person use the pronouns *he, she, it,* and *they*.

Examples: *She* rides the downtown bus. *They* ride the downtown bus.

Refer to the chart below to see how a regular verb changes according to the person of the subject. Note that the only change in the regular verb *ride* is in the third person singular, where *ride* becomes *rides*. Most verbs follow this pattern of adding *-s* or *-es* (see Spelling Rules) to the verb in the third person singular.

	Singular	**Plural**
1st Person	I ride	we ride
2nd Person	you ride	you ride
3rd Person	he, she, it rides	they ride

One verb that you will use often is not regular. It is the verb *be*. Study the following chart to see how this verb changes according to the number and person of the subject. When you write, refer to the chart to be sure that your verb agrees with its subject.

	Singular	**Plural**
1st Person	I am	we are
2nd Person	you are	you are
3rd Person	he, she, it is	they are

Error Number 2: Incorrect Use of the Past Tense

You would be surprised to read these sentences: *He walks yesterday* or *He is home yesterday*. Why? The sentence just sounds wrong to anyone familiar with the English language. The verb in each sentence is in the present tense, yet the sentence refers to a time in the past—*yesterday*. There is a time conflict. Logically, the sentence calls for a verb in the past tense. When you write, make sure that your sentences make sense. Use verbs in the past tense when the action happened in the past.

To make the past tense of regular verbs, such as *walk*, you add -*ed* to the root form of the verb.

Example: He *walked* to the store yesterday.

The chart below shows how to make the past tense of the irregular verb *be*.

	Singular	**Plural**
1st Person	I was	we were
2nd Person	you were	you were
3rd Person	he, she, it was	they were

The chart on page 92 shows the past tense of additional irregular verbs.

Error Number 3: Incorrect Use of the Future Tense

You would also be surprised to read these sentences: *I walked tomorrow* or *She was late tomorrow*. Why? Again, the sentence simply sounds wrong to anyone familiar with the English language. The verbs in both sentences are in the past tense, yet the sentence is referring to a time in the future—*tomorrow*. Logically, the sentences call for a verb in the future tense. Use verbs in the future tense when the action is going to happen in the future.

Forming the future tense of a regular verb is easy. Just add the helping verb *will*.

Example: She *will call* her mother tomorrow.

Forming the future tense of the verb *be* is a little different. You use *will be* for all persons, singular and plural.

Example: I *will be* home tomorrow.

Most of the time in your writing, you will use the present, past, or future tense. But there are other verb tenses that can present problems to any writer. The next two errors occur in the use of the present participle and the past participle.

Error Number 4: Incorrect Use of the Present Participle

Sometimes, in a casual conversation, you may hear a sentence like "You walking home now?" The speaker has chosen to omit the helping verb *are* in his or her question. You know that the sentence means "Are you walking home now?" even without the helping verb. Such omissions are acceptable in everyday speech.

However, when you write, except when you are writing conversations for a story or play, you must include a **helping verb,** a form of the verb *be,* when you use the present-participle form of the verb. The **present participle** is the verb with *-ing* added to it.

Example: I *am planning* a party for their anniversary.

Error Number 5: Incorrect Use of the Past Participle

When you use the past participle, you add a helping verb—*has, have,* or *had*—to the past-participle verb form. In regular verbs, the past participle looks identical to the past tense-form of the verb. Be sure that the helping verb agrees with the number and person of the subject.

Example: The farmer *has picked* all of the beans.
Not: The farmer *have picked* all of the beans.

In some verbs, the past participle looks entirely different from the past-tense form. These verbs are called **irregular**. Be sure to use the correct past-participle form for these irregular verbs.

Example: The birds *have flown* south for the winter.
(*Flown* is the past participle of the verb *fly.*)
Not: The birds have *flied* south for the winter.

Some common irregular verbs are listed in a chart on the next page. Note that some are irregular in their past tense, others are irregular in their past participle, and still others are irregular in both. Refer to the chart when you need help in using the past participle.

Error Number 6: Boring Repetition of a Verb

How would you like it if the sports announcer on the evening news used a particular verb over and over? For example, you might get bored if you heard the announcer say, "The Indians beat the Yankees. The Cubs beat the Pirates. The Blue Jays beat the Tigers." The verb *beat* is used too often. After a while, you begin to tire of it.

You would feel the same way if you read the same verb too many times in a row. When you write, try to avoid repeating a verb. Vary your sentences and make them more interesting by using exciting or unusual verbs.

Example: He *hit* the ball.
He *walloped* the ball.
He *smashed* the ball.
He *creamed* the ball.

IRREGULAR VERBS

Most verbs are **regular.** This usually means that to change from the present tense to the past tense, you simply add the ending -*ed* (*walk—walked*). But some verbs are **irregular,** which means that the past or the past participle—or both—are different. See the spelling rules for more discussion of verbs.

Present	Past	Past Participle
am, is	was	been
are	were	been
bite	bit	bitten
catch	caught	caught
dive	dove	dived
drink	drank	drunk
do	did	done
fly	flew	flown
give	gave	given
go	went	gone
know	knew	known
ring	rang	rung
see	saw	seen
sing	sang	sung
steal	stole	stolen
swim	swam	swum
take	took	taken
wear	wore	worn
write	wrote	written

To demonstrate how irregular some verbs can be, here is a quick summary of most of the kinds of irregular verb changes:

	Present	Past	Past Participle
a. some change all forms	give	gave	given
b. some never change	hit	hit	hit
c. some have the same past tense and past participle	hold	held	held
d. a few change past tense only	run	ran	run

PARTS OF SPEECH

The parts of speech are a way of classifying words.

NOUN: A **noun** is the name of a person, place, or thing. If you can put the word *the* or *a* in front of a word, it is probably a noun.

> *job, hat, dog, man*

Proper nouns are names of a particular person, place, or thing. The important thing to know about proper nouns is that you must capitalize them every time you use them.

> *Mrs. Smith, America, Fido*

Every sentence must have a noun or pronoun.
(See the Capitalization section on page 74.)

PRONOUN: A word used in place of a noun

> *he, you, it, their, someone*

ADJECTIVE: A word that modifies a noun or pronoun

> *green, big, all, those, some*

Note: There is a special kind of adjective called an *article*, and there are only three articles: *the, a,* and *an.*

VERB: A word that shows some kind of action or state

> *run, study, read, is*

Every sentence must have a verb.

ADVERB: A word that modifies a verb, adjective, or adverb

> *quietly, fearfully, very, often, too*

CONJUNCTION: A word used to join words, phrases, or clauses

> *and, or, but, because*

PREPOSITION: A **preposition** is a word used to show the relationship of a noun or pronoun to another word. The combination of the preposition and noun or pronoun is called a **prepositional phrase**. A prepositional phrase acts like an adjective or adverb. The prepositional phrase can modify the noun or pronoun, or a prepositional phrase can modify a verb.

> PREPOSITIONS: *of, from, above, at, to, with*
> PREPOSITIONAL PHRASES: The boy <u>from Arkansas</u> was the first choice <u>for the team.</u>

INTERJECTION: A word that expresses strong emotion
> *Wow! Help! Oh!*

Caution: The same word can be used as different parts of speech. The real determiner is how the word is used in a sentence.

> This is a *light* package. (adjective)
> The *light* is broken. (noun)
> Please *light* the lamp. (verb)
>
> He drives *fast.* (adverb)
> He is a *fast* driver. (adjective)
> The *fast* is over. (noun)

Hint: If you can put an article like *the* in front of a word, you know the word is a noun *(the box)*. A word that comes between the noun and the article *(the <u>big</u> box)* is usually an adjective. Remember that adjectives modify nouns; adverbs modify verbs, adjectives, and adverbs.

ADJECTIVES AND ADVERBS IN COMPARISONS: Adjectives are used to compare things (nouns). Adverbs are used to compare actions (verbs).

To compare one thing with another, use the **comparative form** of the adjective. You make the comparative form of most regular adjectives by adding the ending *-er.* To compare one thing with two or more things, use the **superlative form** of the adjective. You usually make the superlative form by adding the ending *-est.*

high   *Comparative:* higher   *Superlative:* highest

Some adjectives are irregular. Here are their comparative and superlative forms.

good	better	best
bad	worse	worst
many	more	most
little	less	least

You form the comparative and superlative forms of adjectives having two or more syllables by adding *more/most* or *less/least.*

beautiful   *Comparative:* more beautiful   *Superlative:* most beautiful
famous   *Comparative:* less famous   *Superlative:* least famous

For adverbs, follow the same rules as for adjectives.

fast   *Comparative:* faster   *Superlative:* fastest
carefully   *Comparative:* more carefully   *Superlative:* most carefully

GUIDELINES FOR COMPOSITION_____

TYPES OF WRITING

There are many different types of writing. The most obvious way of sorting written works is by form, that is, how the words are arranged on paper. Another way of classifying writing is by the meaning of the words.

Forms of Writing

Prose: In prose, ideas are organized in sentences and paragraphs. When you read it, prose sounds much like normal speech. Most of the writing on this page, and throughout this book, is in prose.

Poetry: In poetry, how the words look and sound is as important as what they say. A poem is organized in lines and groups of lines called **stanzas.** Usually, the arrangement of heavy and light beats in each line follows a pattern. In many poems, lines end in rhyming words. Here is an example of a rhyming poem:

> *Red sky at night,*
> *Sailors' delight.*
> *Red in the morning,*
> *Sailors take warning.*

Drama: Usually, a drama or play is written to be acted. In written form, the typical play begins with a list of the characters and a description of the scene. Then the words of the play are arranged according to which character says them, as in this example:

> CHRIS: Where's Maria?
> SANTO: In the garden.
> CHRIS: Now? In this downpour?

There is some overlapping of forms. For example, in a drama the characters' words are written in either prose or poetry.

Written works within each form can be subdivided into smaller groups. Poems, for example, can be sorted into those that use rhyme and those that do not; the rhyming poems can then be sorted according to their patterns of rhymes. Prose pieces are often grouped according to whether they are about facts or imagined things.

Nonfiction and Fiction

Nonfiction: Nonfiction refers to prose writing that discusses ideas or real people, places, things, and events. The order that a writer uses in a nonfiction work depends on the work and its purpose. For example, in a description of a specific dinosaur, a scientist might begin with the skeleton and work outward, or with the head and work back to the tail. In an explanation of why dinosaurs died out, the scientist might present the most likely reasons and work down to lesser possibilities. A discussion of the different ages in which dinosaurs lived would follow time order. A thorough report on dinosaurs might have several different sections, each one following a different order.

Here are some of the many types of nonfiction:

- Letters, both personal and business
- Business plans and proposals
- Reports in all fields of study, including history, geography, the fine arts, and the sciences
- Biography—an account of a real person's life, written by someone else
- Autobiography—an account of a real person's life, written by that person
- Newspaper articles about current events
- Descriptions of people, animals, places, and other things
- Directions for an activity
- Essays stating opinions and/or attempting to persuade readers to accept certain ideas or take certain actions
- Humorous essays

Fiction: Fiction refers to stories (usually in prose) that come from a writer's imagination. Characters and events in a work of fiction may be based on real people and happenings, but the writer adds or changes the material for a more interesting story. In fiction, events are usually discussed in chronological, or time, order.

There are many subgroups within fiction, such as these:

- Realistic fiction—stories that tell about things that could really happen, with believable characters and accurate settings. Generally, realistic stories are set in our own time.
- Historical fiction—stories based on people and events in history. These stories are based on nonfiction reports and descriptions written during the era in which the story is set.
- Science fiction—stories that consider how new inventions or scientific discoveries may change our way of life. All of the details in a science fiction story should be in agreement with science as we understand it now.
- Fantasy—tales that involve magic, imaginary creatures, or similar unreal elements. Happenings in a fantasy do not need to be in agreement with normal life.
- Folktales—stories shared by being told and retold. Folktales change slightly in the retelling but keep the details and ideas that are important to the people who share the story.

THE WRITING PROCESS

At many times throughout your life you will want to write something special, perhaps for a class, a news article, or a speech. You will want your writing to be good enough that you will feel proud to have others, even strangers, read it. Few people write well on the first try. Writing is a process that takes time and care. There are five stages in the writing process: prewriting, writing, revising, proofreading, and sharing.

First, you need to think, to plan, and to gather and organize ideas (Stage One—Prewriting). Then you get your ideas down on paper (Stage Two—Writing a First Draft). After you have written the first draft, it is time to review your work to be sure it makes sense and presents the material in the most effective way possible (Stage Three—Revising). Next, you make simple corrections to spelling, grammar, and punctuation (Stage Four—Proofreading). Finally, you produce an attractive finished copy, ready for your readers to enjoy (Stage Five—Sharing).

On the following pages are some ideas that will help you in each of the five stages of writing. Remember that, no matter what kind of writing you do, the steps are the same.

STAGE 1: PREWRITING: GET READY TO WRITE

Few writers know exactly what they want to say before they begin. During the prewriting stage they plan, gather ideas, and organize their findings.

1. **Choose a topic.** You may find it helpful to keep a journal while you are working on a writing project. Jot down ideas as they occur to you. If you happen to see something that relates to a possible writing topic, record your impressions right away. Try to write in the journal every day. When you have to come up with an original idea for something to write about, you may find a topic in your journal.

   Try brainstorming to find a good topic. Some people like to talk over their ideas with friends. Often, just bouncing your thoughts off others will help you come up with topics you might not have discovered on your own. If no one else is around, try jotting down topics that come to mind, not judging their worth at this point. Later, you can reread the list and choose the topic you like best.

   You might have several possibilities for a report. If you can't decide on one topic, try making a cluster graph for each of your possible topics. (See page 116 for an illustration.) First, write each topic on a page and draw a circle around it. Then cluster other related words or questions around the circled topic. By the time you have finished filling up the paper with ideas that are related to the topic in the circle, you will have many thoughts to write about. Choose the topic for which the ideas come most easily. That is probably the one in which you are most interested.

2. **Decide on a purpose.** Are you writing to explain a difficult topic? Do you want to entertain your audience with humor or human interest stories? Is your purpose to persuade readers to think a certain way? Do you want to share your feelings with readers? Decide why you are writing and what you want your writing to accomplish.

3. **Think about your audience.** Various audiences expect and enjoy different kinds of writing. Someone reading a research report expects a serious approach, whereas a person reading a magazine article might be looking for light entertainment. You'll need to keep your audience in mind as you write.

4. **Gather information about your topic.** Use any possible source to learn more about your topic. Reference books such as encyclopedias are excellent places to begin your search when you are writing a report. Another place to check is a book that focuses entirely on your topic. Keep an atlas, an almanac, and a dictionary handy. Magazines are also helpful, as are on-line computer searches that can give you up-to-the-minute information.

   Sometimes the best source of information is a person who knows the topic well. Interview a parent, a teacher, a student, or someone else in the community with personal knowledge of, or experience with, your subject. Prepare a list of questions in advance. Be sure to take good notes so you can read them later.

5. **Arrange your ideas.** A report is not simply a listing of all the notes you took. You will find that some of the notes you took are important, while others no longer match your topic. Throw out the ones that don't belong. Then arrange the remaining notes in an order that will make sense to your readers. Many writers make a formal or informal outline at this point. A report may be arranged in time order or in logical order, depending on the topic. A story is usually organized in time order. The most effective way to organize a description is to arrange the details in a visual way, for example, from top to bottom or from left to right. Reasons in a persuasive piece might be arranged in order of importance, from least important to most important. See pages 116 through 118 for more information on how to organize various types of writing.

STAGE 2: WRITING A FIRST DRAFT: PUT YOUR IDEAS ON PAPER OR ON A COMPUTER SCREEN

Now that you have gone through the prewriting stage, you have a topic, some notes, and an outline of some sort. That's a good start, but what do you do about that empty piece of paper in front of you? That's easy—just start writing! Now is the time to get your ideas down on paper. Not all of the words may be spelled right. Try to follow your outline as much as possible, but don't be a slave to it. If new ideas occur to you, include them, even if some of your thoughts may be out of order. Later, in the revising and proofreading stages, you will improve what you have written and will correct any mistakes. It is a good idea to write only on every other line so that you will have plenty of room to make changes later. If you are using a word processor or computer, it will be easy to revise your writing.

   When you are beginning to write, sometimes you need a little push to get started. If you're having trouble getting under way, try one of the following ideas. Some of these suggestions are useful for many different kinds of writing.

1. **Begin with a question.** During the prewriting stage, you gathered a lot of information and details. Read over your notes and come up with a question that may have entered your mind during your research, such as, "How would you like to be a salesclerk in a department store?" That sentence can be the first sentence in your introduction. Then use your notes to explain the role of a salesclerk in the paragraphs that form the body of your writing.

2. **Begin by making a statement about a character.** For example, if you were writing a story, you could begin with "There was a grouchy salesclerk with bright red hair who enjoyed being rude to her customers."

3. **Begin by having the main character speak.** To begin a story, you might write this: *"Help you find the right size? No way! I'm busy," said the red-haired clerk.*

4. **Open with your opinion.** Write as though you were talking to a friend. You could begin with a sentence like this: *When someone comes into a store to spend money, he or she should at least be treated with common courtesy.*

5. **Start with a simile.** Compare unlike things, using the words *like* or *as*. Here are two examples: *The huge store stands like a fort* and *Her hair was as bright as a stoplight.* A **metaphor** compares two unlike things without using the words *like* or *as*. Here is an example of a metaphor: *The huge store was a fort.* See pages 124 through 127 for additional writing techniques.

6. When you don't know where to begin or what to say next, you have what is called **writer's block.** One way to break the block is to **write your name over and over.** Do this until an idea pops into your mind. You'll be surprised at how quickly another idea will come when you keep your writing hand moving.

7. Another way to break a writer's block is to **rearrange what you have already written.** Often the place where you are stuck is not really the problem. You may have made a wrong turn a few paragraphs back, and now you are at a dead end. The only way out of a dead end is to go back to the place where you made the wrong turn. By rearranging what you are writing, you can locate the trouble spot.

8. Sometimes, you may know exactly how to end your writing, but not how to begin it. **Remember that writing does not always have to be done in order,** from beginning to end. Occasionally, it is easier to write the end or the middle before you tackle the beginning. Begin wherever you can. You can always rearrange your work later. Just keep in mind that your final draft should follow your outline as closely as possible. If you want to change your outline at any point, go right ahead. But then follow the revised outline.

STAGE 3: REVISING: IMPROVE YOUR WRITING

Now it is time to revise your writing. When you revise, your goal is to find ways to make your writing better. Rereading what you have written is an important step in revising. Ask yourself if your writing has met your purpose. Read it from the point of view of your audience. Will they understand and enjoy your writing? Now examine your choice of words. You will probably need to cross out some words and write in new ones. Check to see that you have made your writing lively and interesting by using the best words and sentence structures. Maybe you will want to draw arrows to show where words or sentences should be moved. Writers often make revisions in a pencil or pen of another color. Don't worry about your writing looking messy at this point. You will make it look neat again later when you present your work as a finished product. If you use a word processor or a computer, you have a choice. You can revise right on the screen, or you can get a printout and mark it up in the traditional way.

Next, read what you have written (and, possibly, revised) to a partner. Ask him or her which part is best and whether there is anything he or she would like to know more about. Ask whether the organization of ideas is clear and makes sense. Find out if your partner can offer any suggestions. Then make more changes, if you think the changes will improve what you have written. As you revise, you may want to check off the appropriate items on the revision checklist below.

Revision Checklist

_____ 1. **Did I meet my purpose?**

Story

_____ Are the events in my story arranged in time order so readers understand what happened first, second, and last?

_____ Did I create realistic characters?

_____ Did I write believable dialogue?

_____ If I wrote a fantasy, does my story contain enough details to make the reader want to believe the impossible?

Instructions

_____ Are the steps in the directions arranged in time order so readers understand what to do first, second, and last?

_____ Did I include all the steps that are necessary? Did I skip any?

_____ Are all the steps I included absolutely necessary for the process? Should any be deleted?

Biography

_____ Are the events in the subject's life presented in a clear time order?

_____ Did I include enough details to bring the subject to life in the reader's mind? Do the details put the person in a particular place and time?

Description

_____ Did I arrange details in spatial order, helping my readers move from one location to the next?

_____ Did I include enough sensory details to create a picture in the reader's mind?

Persuasive Writing

_____ Did I state my opinion clearly?

_____ Did I arrange my arguments in order of importance, from least to most important?

_____ Did I offer facts and logical reasons to support my opinions?

Report

_____ Does the report have an introduction, body paragraphs, and a conclusion?

_____ Are the ideas organized logically or in time order, depending on my topic?

_____ Does each paragraph in my report have a topic sentence that expresses the main idea?

_____ Do all the sentences in every paragraph of my report develop the main idea?

_____ 2. **Have I used words and sentences as effectively as possible?**

_____ Did I put too many ideas in one sentence? Can I improve any sentences by breaking them into two sentences?

_____ Are my sentences too short and choppy? Can I improve my writing by combining any sentences?

_____ Did I vary the type of sentence I used? (Varying sentences' length and pattern helps to keep your writing lively and interesting.)

_____ Have I used signal words such as *in addition, however, next, for example, while, different from,* and *in conclusion* to help my readers follow my line of thinking?

_____ Did the words I chose help to create a particular mood? Would other words, similes, and metaphors contribute more effectively to the mood I want to create?

_____ Are there more exact or stronger words that I could use? (A thesaurus is a good place to find words having similar meanings.)

_____ Did I overuse any words? Did I overuse common adjectives, such as *good, bad,* and *nice?* (Look in a thesaurus or a dictionary for alternatives.)

_____ Did I use adjectives and adverbs that form sharp word pictures?

_____ Did I use adverbs to give information about *how, when,* and *where* to make my meaning clear?

_____ Should I replace some nouns with pronouns to add variety?

_____ Did I use active verbs whenever possible? (Passive verbs can take the life out of most writing.)

_____ Did I use any literary techniques such as similes or metaphors? (See pages 124 to 127 for further explanation.)

STAGE 4: PROOFREADING: FIND AND FIX THE ERRORS

Now that you have checked to see that what you have written says what you want it to say, it is time to proofread your work. When you proofread, you look for simple errors in grammar, punctuation, capitalization, and spelling. Proofreading is important. A carefully presented piece of writing shows that you care about your subject and about your reader. Readers are much more likely to understand and appreciate your writing if they don't have to overlook careless errors.

Look for only one type of error at a time. For example, you might look for spelling errors first. Later you can look for other kinds of errors in grammar, capitalization, and punctuation.

When you proofread, it is a good idea to put a sheet of paper or a ruler under each line as you read it. That way, you will be more likely to find any mistakes. Some people find it easier to spot spelling errors if they read each line backward, not allowing the sense of the words to cause them to overlook a misspelling.

Writers often have trouble seeing their own mistakes. Let someone else proofread what you have written. It is usually easier to spot someone else's errors. Another way to spot mistakes is to read your writing aloud to a friend. This method often uncovers places where words were omitted or ideas were poorly worded.

When you find an error in your writing, mark it with a proofreading symbol. A list of proofreading symbols appears on page 104.

The proofreading checklist on the next page will help you find your errors.

Proofreading Checklist

_____ 1. Are all the groups of words complete sentences? Does each group of words have a subject and a predicate? (page 84)

_____ 2. Do the verbs agree with the subjects of the sentences? (page 89)

_____ 3. Was I careful when forming the past tense and past participle of irregular verbs? (pages 90–92)

_____ 4. Did I spell words correctly? (Use the Spelling Checker on pages 9–66.)

_____ 5. Did I capitalize correctly? (page 74)

_____ 6. Did I use the correct punctuation mark at the end of each sentence? (pages 76–77)

_____ 7. Did I put commas in the correct places? (page 77)

_____ 8. Did I use apostrophes correctly? (pages 78–79)

_____ 9. Did I indent each paragraph?

STAGE 5: SHARING: LETTING OTHERS READ WHAT YOU HAVE WRITTEN

After you finish proofreading, it is time to let your audience read your writing. Writing that is interesting and correct deserves to be presented attractively so that the audience will naturally want to read it.

If you have written your report by hand, copy it neatly and make sure your words are easy to read. You may even want to skip every other line to make your writing look less crowded. If you have worked on a computer, run a final spelling check. Remember, however, that a spelling check doesn't scan for sense and so will not spot a homonym used incorrectly, for example, *there* instead of *their*. After checking for homonym errors, print out a good copy of your work, preferably double-spaced. No matter how you present your final copy, be sure to give your writing a title to let the reader know what to expect. Keep in mind that the addition of charts, graphs, and photographs will add to your readers' understanding and enjoyment of your work, especially if it is a report.

Some other ways to share your work include the following:

* Post your writing on a bulletin board for friends to read.

* Read your writing into an audio tape recorder. In this way, you can share your work with those who may not have an opportunity to read your final copy.

* Get together with other writers and assemble a booklet of reports or other kinds of writing. You can decide what to include based on a type of writing chosen, such as reports, poems, or stories; or the selections might be based on a theme, such as friendship, the natural world, or technology.

PROOFREADING SYMBOLS

Use these symbols to mark places where you want to make changes and corrections in your first draft.

Notation in Margin	How Indicated in Copy	Explanation
¶	true. The best rule to follow	New paragraph
⌒	living room	close up
#	Mary hada	Insert space
∿	Mary had a lamb little	Transpose
sp	There were ⑤ children	Spell out
cap	mary had a little lamb	Capitalize
lc	Mary had a little Lamb	Lower case
e	The correct proceedure	Delete or take out
stet	Mary had a little lamb	Restore crossed-out word(s)
little	Mary had a lamb	Insert word(s) in margin
⊙	Birds fly	Insert a period
⌃	Next the main	Insert a comma

THE PARAGRAPH

There's more to writing a good paragraph than just stringing together a bunch of sentences. In an effective paragraph, the sentences work together to develop a single idea, called the **main idea**.

Often the main idea is stated in one sentence, called the **topic sentence**. Then the rest of the sentences add details or support to it. Writers often try to place the topic sentence first or last in the paragraph, but it may appear in any position. Here is an example of a paragraph with a topic sentence.

> Electric vehicles do not produce any dangerous or dirty exhaust fumes. <u>However, electric cars may not be the answer to our pollution problems.</u> These cars cannot go very far or very fast. Their batteries must be recharged after only four or so hours of use, and the recharging may take six hours or more. Worse yet, the electricity that recharges the batteries comes from power plants that produce pollution. In effect, the pollution is merely moved from one source to another.

Other times, the reader must combine the bits of information in all of the sentences to decide what the main idea is. The following paragraph has a main idea but no topic sentence. After reading the paragraph, try to state its main idea in a sentence or phrase.

> A good guide to the city must, of course, know a great deal about the history, buildings, and people of the city. He or she must be able to discuss each important site as it comes into view of the tour group. A sense of humor is another necessity, along with a great deal of patience. In addition, it helps if a guide speaks several languages fluently.

When you write a paragraph, make sure that you don't confuse your reader with sentences that are off the topic. Compare the paragraph above with this one:

> A good guide to the city must, of course, know a great deal about the history, buildings, and people of the city. Some cities are more interesting to visit than others. The guide must be able to discuss each important site as it comes into view of the tour group. When the tour group is on a bus with a good sound system, the passengers can hear the guide better. A sense of humor is another necessity, along with a great deal of patience. In addition, it helps if a guide speaks several languages fluently. The only language I speak is English.

Most readers like paragraphs that are not too long. Try to make your point in three to six sentences. To make each paragraph interesting, avoid beginning every sentence with the same word, such as *The*. Whenever possible, vary the sentence patterns. For example, the sentences in the paragraph you are reading now begin with a subject, a verb, an infinitive, and two modifying phrases.

FRIENDLY LETTER FORM: THANK-YOU NOTE

A friendly letter is a good way to maintain relationships with friends and relatives. Friendly letters follow a particular, accepted form. A thank-you note follows the same form as a friendly letter, only it is much shorter. When you receive a gift or a friend does you a favor, you write a thank-you note. You name the gift or favor you have received and make the person feel that the present or favor is quite special.

HEADING	167 George Road Detroit, MI 08022 January 12, 1997
GREETING	Dear Aunt Laverne,
BODY	Thank you for the beautiful bathroom towels you sent for my new apartment. How thoughtful of you! They match the wall color perfectly, as you will see when you come over. I hope to see you soon and thank you in person.
CLOSING	Your niece,
SIGNATURE	Marcella

Like a friendly letter, a thank-you note starts with a **heading** that states your address and the date. Be sure to put a comma between the city and state and between the day of the month and the year.

The first word of the **greeting** is usually *Dear*. Notice that it begins with a capital letter. The word(s) after the greeting is the name of the person receiving the letter, and it is followed by a comma.

The part of the note where you say thank you is called the **body.** In a friendly letter, this is where you write your news or message. The first word of every paragraph is indented.

The **closing** signals the end of the note or letter. Notice that only the first word is capitalized, and a comma follows the last word.

The closing lines up with the heading and **signature,** which is your name.

BUSINESS LETTER FORM

When you wish to order something through the mail, ask for permission, or get some information, you write a business letter. Unlike a friendly letter, a business letter has an inside address and uses a colon after the greeting instead of a comma.

320 20th Avenue Menomonie, WI 54751 January 14, 1997	HEADING
Ms. Heather Kistler, Director Arkansas Department of Tourism Little Rock, Arkansas 72201	INSIDE ADDRESS
Dear Ms. Kistler:	GREETING
My family and I are planning to take a camping trip this summer. Please send me a state map and some information about campgrounds and places to see. Right now we are interested in the Hot Springs National Park area. Information about other noteworthy parts of the state will help us decide what else to visit.	BODY
Yours truly,	CLOSING
Kara Zola	SIGNATURE

A business letter starts with a **heading.** It gives your address and the date. Notice that there is a comma between the city and state and between the day of the month and the year.

The **inside address** gives the name, title, and address of the person to whom you are writing as well as the name of the organization or company. Remember to put a comma between the person's name and title, and be sure to capitalize the title.

The **greeting** is followed by a colon (:) in a business letter. Then comes the **body** or content of the letter.

In the **closing,** only the first word is capitalized, and a comma follows the last word. In a business letter, you can close with *Respectfully, Sincerely, Yours truly*, or *Very truly yours.*

The closing and the **signature,** which is the writer's name, line up with the heading. Add your position after the signature if it is appropriate. For example:

Joe Smith
Asst. Manager

Add enclosures, if any, at the bottom after the signature. For example:

Enclosed, two photographs

WRITING A STORY AND WRITING ABOUT A STORY

All stories, from folktales to novels, share certain elements. The examples below of these elements are drawn from the folktale "Little Red Riding Hood."

- **Setting:** Where and when the story takes place

  time—an imaginary time long ago; place—in a forest

- **Characters:** Who is in the story. Possible characters include people, animals, and imaginary beings.

  a little girl, her mother and grandmother, a talking wolf, and a woodsman

- **Conflict:** A problem or struggle that must be settled in the course of the story. The conflict may be between two characters, between characters and nature, or between two desires within a single character.

  The wolf tries to eat Little Red Riding Hood.

- **Plot:** The series of events that shows how the conflict begins, builds, and is resolved, or settled. The plot usually has these stages:

Introduction This stage presents the setting, introduces the main characters, and shows the beginning of the conflict.

From a house in the forest, a mother sends her daughter out with goodies for her sick grandmother, warning the girl to avoid strangers. The girl meets a wolf.

Rising Action The conflict grows more serious.

The wolf runs ahead of the girl to her grandmother's home. He swallows the grandmother and dresses in her clothing. When the girl arrives, the wolf tries to convince her that he is the grandmother and that she should come close to him.

Climax The conflict reaches a point where one of the conflicting forces must change course. Usually, this is the most exciting moment of the story.

The wolf declares that he will eat the girl, and he jumps at her. The girl screams.

Falling Action The results of the change become clear. The conflict winds down.

The woodsman rushes in to help the girl. He strikes the wolf with his ax and kills him. The grandmother then jumps out, whole and safe.

Resolution All the loose ends of the story are tied up.

The girl delivers her goodies. The humans all live happily ever after.

Writing an Original Story

As you plan a story, you may find the following form helpful. It is called a **story map**. Jot down your ideas for each element of the story. Then use the map as an outline, or guide, as you write the story.

STORY MAP

Title: _____

Setting: Where _____ When _____

Characters (Briefly describe each main character.): _____

_____

Conflict: _____

Stages and Events in Plot:

1. Introduction _____

2. Rising Action _____

   _____

3. Climax _____

4. Falling Action _____

   _____

5. Resolution _____

Writing About a Story

Sometimes you may be asked to retell or summarize a story. Use the story map above to help you identify the important parts of the story. Then, if you write about each story part, your summary will be complete.

Other times you may be asked to report on a story or book and give your opinion of it. The form below will help you organize your thoughts.

BOOK REPORT

Title: _____

Author: _____

What is the book about? Who? Where? When?

_____

Who is your favorite or least favorite character? Why?

_____

What is your opinion of the book? Why?

_____

Do you recommend this book? If so, to whom? Why?

_____

KEEPING A DAILY JOURNAL

A daily journal is like a diary. The difference is that you don't write anything secret or private in it the way you might in a diary. Many writers view the journal as their best friend. It's a place where you can do the following:

- jot down an idea

- experiment with writing

- write a creative story or poem

- expand your vocabulary by writing down new words you like

- practice writing every day

- record an impression

- write about how you feel at a particular time

- tell your reaction to what is happening around you

- write down an opinion of a book, a movie, or a piece of music

Your recorded thoughts can serve as a source of ideas for writing at a later time. You will often write about things in your journal that you may want to share with others.

Tips for Writing in Your Journal

1. Date each entry.

2. Begin by writing three to five minutes a day. Move up gradually to ten minutes a day.

3. Write when you feel relaxed, if possible.

4. Don't worry about spelling or punctuation. The important thing is that you are writing and getting ideas down on paper.

5. When doing creative writing, you could try out one of the ideas on the "Things To Write About in Your Journal" list on the next page, or you might want to use a story starter. See page 119 for some more ideas.

6. Write in complete sentences when you put down your thoughts.

7. Use action verbs and the present tense to keep your writing lively.

8. Use adjectives and adverbs to give a clear picture.

Things To Write About in Your Journal

1. Write about your hobby or something you would like to do as a hobby.

2. Discuss the history of your state, city, neighborhood, or family.

3. Describe what you think is the best thing about living today. Describe the worst thing.

4. Write about the ways raising a child today is different from how it was fifty years ago.

5. Vent stored-up anger or frustration by writing about something that's been troubling you.

6. Find a picture that you like. React to it in your journal.

7. Write about something you have just learned or heard about.

8. Discuss the reasons you like or dislike sports.

9. Describe your favorite quiet place. Jot down what you think about when you are there.

10. Write about a beach or lake shore near your home or one you've visited. What have you found when you have combed the beach?

11. Write a letter of appreciation to someone, living or dead, who has had a positive effect on your life. Begin with "Dear . . ." and keep writing.

12. Record your impressions about something that happened at work.

WRITING INSTRUCTIONS

You read instructions almost every day. When you follow a recipe, you read all the steps it takes to make a specific dish. When you work on a car, you often need to read instructions from a manual. You yourself will often write instructions that explain how to do something. It's almost certain that someday you will need to write down directions to your house or to explain how to care for your pet while you are away. Everyone needs to know how to write explanations and instructions.

Tips for Writing Instructions

1. Before you begin to write, think about the order of steps. Try to picture yourself performing the task. What do you do first, second, third, last? Jot down the steps as they occur to you. Then go over the steps carefully to see if you forgot anything.

2. On the same sheet of paper, number the main steps of the job. You will follow this informal outline when you write your first draft.

3. Begin with a topic sentence that lets readers know which task or skill you are about to explain. Let the topic sentence give the reader an idea of your attitude toward the subject. An example would be, "Making a chocolate torte takes time and patience, but it's worth the effort."

4. Follow your outline as you write your first draft. Add any details that you feel are necessary.

5. Have a friend read the instructions when you think they are perfect. See if he or she can understand what to do. Ask if your friend has any suggestions about how to improve the directions. Revise the paragraph after you decide which changes should be made.

Topics for Instructions

1. Explain how to get from your house to a local landmark or public building.

2. Explain how to cook a favorite dish or ethnic specialty.

3. Explain how to adjust the brakes on a mountain bicycle.

4. Explain how to do a particular dance step.

5. Explain how to set up a tent.

WRITING A NEWS ARTICLE

You may one day have an opportunity to report on an event for a newsletter or newspaper. Newswriting is different in many ways from other types of writing. News articles must be written to be understood quickly because people don't want to spend much time reading them. Because readers often don't even bother to read the whole article, the important ideas and facts about the event must be presented in the first few paragraphs. News articles give just the facts, and they do it in as few words as possible.

Tips for Writing a News Article

1. Before you begin to write, gather all the facts you can about the topic. Try to answer these questions: *who, what, when, where, why,* and *how?* Keep a reporter's notebook handy when you interview witnesses or experts. Don't rely on your memory. News articles must be accurate.

2. Organize your notes in time order. What happened first, second, third, last? Now study your notes again. Which details are needed for a quick understanding of the event? Mark the facts that are most important.

3. Write a title for the article that includes both a subject and a verb. The verb always is written in the present tense. An example would be, "Internet Offers Wealth of Info on Candidates."

4. Your first few sentences should answer the questions *who, what, when, where, why,* and *how.* The later paragraphs can explain and describe the event in greater detail. Keep in mind that if there isn't enough room on the page, the editor will delete paragraphs from the bottom up.

5. Double-check your article for accuracy. Pay special attention to names, places, dates, and times.

Topics for News Articles

1. Report on a meeting of the local school board.

2. Report on a fair or festival.

3. Report on the campaign of a candidate running for office.

4. Report on a football or basketball game.

5. Report on a natural disaster, such as a storm or a fire.

WRITING TO DESCRIBE

A good description paints a picture in the reader's mind. When you write a description, include details that appeal to all the senses—sight, hearing, taste, touch, and smell. You can re-create the sight of a mountain stream, the sounds of a city street, the taste of a lemon tart, the feel of a cat's fur, and the smell of an apple pie for your reader by carefully choosing the best words.

Tips for Writing a Description

1. Before you begin to write, print the name of your topic in a central circle on a sheet of paper and then draw five lines radiating from the circle, one for each sense. For each sense, jot down words or phrases that describe the topic. Refer to this diagram later when you write your first draft.

2. Organize your ideas and details. Arrange your details in a spatial way, that is, describing each detail in relation to the ones near it. In this way, you logically lead the reader from one part of the object or scene to the next.

3. Begin with a topic sentence that lets readers know what you are about to describe.

4. Use exact nouns, strong verbs, and lively adjectives and adverbs. Show the reader what you see, smell, hear, touch, and taste by including clear and specific details.

Topics for Descriptions

1. Describe a favorite place from your childhood.

2. Describe the feel of foods in your refrigerator if you explored inside it with your eyes closed.

3. Describe a memorable holiday—the sights, the sounds, the smells, and the tastes that make it special.

4. Describe a particular room that you know well, for example, your bedroom or living room.

5. Describe the sights and sounds of a typical morning in your home.

6. Describe your favorite meal or dessert.

7. Describe a musical concert.

8. Describe the passengers you might see on a bus in your city or town.

WRITING TO PERSUADE

Sometimes you are faced with issues and questions about which you have definite opinions. Perhaps you believe that your city's health department should do more to protect babies from childhood illnesses. Maybe you agree or disagree with an article you read in the local newspaper. It may be that a conflict has come up between union workers and management, and you believe your point of view should be heard. In these cases, you can write a letter that will present arguments to support your opinion.

Tips for Writing To Persuade

1. Research your topic. Find out what other people are thinking and saying about the issue. Be sure you have your facts correct before you begin.

2. Plan your arguments carefully. Do not begin writing until you have a clear understanding of your point of view on the subject.

3. Consider your audience. Decide which of the facts and which of your opinions to include based on who you think will read your letter and whom you want to persuade.

4. State your point of view clearly at the start. Begin by telling your readers what you believe and what you want *them* to believe. This is often the right time to explain the opposing side's point of view. Later, you can show why you are right and they are wrong.

5. Arrange each of your reasons in order. Usually, the reasons are arranged in order of importance, from least to most important. This type of organization leaves the reader with the strongest argument last.

6. One by one, develop each argument by including such details as facts, figures, and real-life examples.

7. Write a strong conclusion. Restate the most important point of your arguments and your own opinion. Finally, suggest action that the convinced reader should take.

Topics To Write About Using Persuasive Writing

1. Write to your congressperson about your opinion on a bill or law that is under consideration.

2. Write to a business about your stand on hiring practices, their return policy, or their selling tactics.

3. Write to a newspaper's Letters to the Editor column explaining your opinion on the way the local schools are run—positive or negative.

TECHNIQUES FOR COMPOSITION

WAYS OF ORGANIZING YOUR THOUGHTS

Sometimes when you prepare to write, you have only a dim idea of what you want to say. You don't know how to build that thought into a meaningful piece of writing. Other times you have many facts and ideas in mind. You aren't sure that all of them are needed, or how to pull them together. Here are some suggestions for dealing with both problems.

Building on a Single Thought

Brainstorming Write down your general topic, such as *Careers*. Then, by yourself or with the help of others, note all of the other topics that come to mind when you think about that first topic. List the new topics without judging them. As you do this, you may find natural ways of grouping the topics, but don't work at it. When you run dry, read over the list and choose a topic you would like to work with.

> Example: <u>Careers</u>
> Scientist
> Doctor—Physician's Assistant—Nurse—Medical Secretary
> Police Officer
> Dog Trainer

Cluster Graph Write your topic on a sheet of paper and circle it. Draw several lines leading out from the circle. At the end of each line, write a word or phrase related to the topic. Circle each of these related items, and repeat the process as many times as you can. Then examine your graph and select the parts that are most interesting to you.

Example:

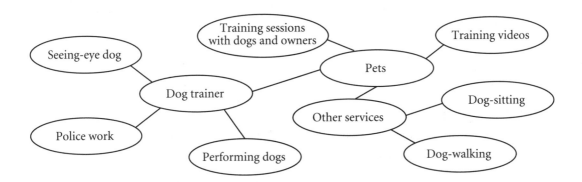

Categorizing After you have identified several facts or ideas you want to develop, examine what you have. Decide on several **categories,** or ways of grouping the information. Make a chart with several columns. Head each column with a word or phrase that describes a category. List each fact or idea in an appropriate box. Jot down your questions and suggestions to yourself, too. Soon you will see what information you still need in order to write about the topic.

Example:

Job Description	Training	Where to look for jobs	Comments
Giving dogs (and owners) basic training	—courses at private businesses —schools?	—all over country —Can you do this as freelance trainer, or only with an agency?	Maybe interview Janet about her job experiences
Dog-sitting; dog-walking	none	—all over country —advertise on flyers, bulletin boards, etc.	
Training dogs to perform	?	—agencies that work with TV, movie producers —circuses?	Can Yellow Pages help here?
Making videos on dog training	video production	—video production houses —as freelancer?	

Putting Thoughts into Order

Chronological, or Time, Order Use this order to organize events in fictional stories and in nonfiction reports of real events; use it also to list steps in how-to articles and explanations of processes. Using **chronological order** means relating events in the order in which they happen. When you are organizing many facts, a time line may help.

Example:

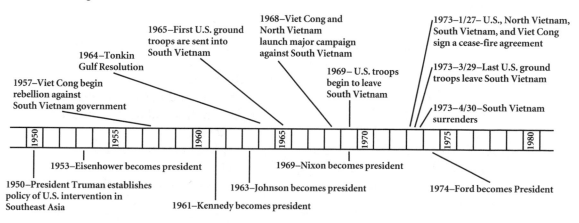

Spatial Order Use this order to list details in a description. Using **spatial order** means arranging details about a thing in the order in which an observer would notice them. For example, you could describe a room from ceiling to floor, or vice versa; from left to right; from the walls to the center; or from the most noticeable piece of furniture to the things around it.

Logical Order Use this order in writing that explains or persuades. Using **logical order** means presenting facts or ideas in such a way that each builds on what has come before. There are many different approaches, such as these:

- **order of importance** Present the least important reason first and the most important reason last (or vice versa). For example, you could present arguments in favor of home schooling in increasing order of importance.
- **comparison and contrast** Describe characteristics of one thing and then the characteristics of a second thing. Show how the things are alike or different. For example, you might use comparison and contrast to show what traditional schooling and home schooling have in common and how they differ.
- **cause-effect** Identify an event or a condition and then discuss how certain actions led to it. For example, you might discuss a system of year-round schooling used in a particular district. First, you could describe the school calendar. Next, you could identify the reasons the school administration chose the present schedule. You might then focus on overcrowding, objections to long summer vacations, and efforts to improve education.
- **problem-solution** Identify a problem and then present steps that can be taken to solve it. You might, for example, show that computer equipment in your school district is outdated. Then you would propose ways of bringing together students and high-tech equipment.

Outlining Whichever order you choose for organizing facts and ideas, you may find it helpful to use an informal or formal outline to plan your writing. The outline lets you see where you are going. Then, as you write, you are less likely to get bogged down or to stray from the subject.

Examples:

INFORMAL OUTLINE	FORMAL OUTLINE
A Brief History of the Vietnam War	A Brief History of the Vietnam War
Introductory paragraph	I. Introduction
Background	II. Setting the Stage
— Truman policy	A. Truman and the Korean War
— Eisenhower policy	B. Eisenhower and the Domino Theory
The war	III. The Conflict
— Events of Kennedy's administration	A. Kennedy and the "Advisors"
— Events of Johnson's administration	B Johnson
— Events of Nixon's administration	1. Tonkin Gulf Resolution
Aftereffects of the war	2. Open U.S. involvement
	(and so on)

STORY STARTERS

INTERESTING TITLES

The Me That Nobody Knows

The Tallest Tale of All

My Best Quality

The Perfect Gift

Abducted by Aliens

A Family Reunion

Winning the Lottery

My Personal Hero

I Had the Strangest Dream

A Perfect Date

My Pet Peeve

Emergency!

In the Dark

The Spectacular Game

A Shopper's Paradise

The Lost Suitcase

The Sleepless Night

My Fifteen Minutes of Fame

The Baby Checks In

Bad News

The Midnight Visitor

A Stress-Filled Day

My Fantasy Vacation

My Natural Highs

My Big Dream

An Extra Place at the Table

OPENERS

- I'd give anything to meet . . .
- I won't be at class for the rest of the year because . . .
- My favorite childhood experience was . . .
- When I start my new job, I'll . . .
- The most valuable thing my parents taught me was . . .
- The best day of my life was when . . .
- The worst day of my life was when . . .
- If I could be anybody, I'd like to be . . .
- If I were invited to write for a television show, I'd write scripts for . . .
- With my children, I'll never . . .
- My New Year's resolution will be . . .
- My child is special because . . .
- When I go on vacation, I'll . . .
- A major turning point in my life was . . .
- My worst nightmare was . . .
- My goal in life is to . . .
- I just bought a new . . .
- My favorite time of day is . . .
- The day I picked up my new . . .
- My favorite song makes me feel . . .
- I like the (your favorite) music group because . . .
- Nothing ever scared me more than . . .
- One thing that really bothers me is . . .
- When the door burst open, . . .
- My most prized possession is . . .
- My favorite author is . . .
- My favorite book is . . .
- The most exciting thing that ever happened at work was . . .
- The last good movie I saw was . . .
- My favorite comic strip character is . . .
- I would like to be . . .
- Holidays (or name a specific holiday) make(s) me feel . . .
- I can hardly wait to . . .

GOOD QUESTIONS

- What do you think are the worst driving habits?
- How is watching a game on television different from attending one in person?
- Whom would you like to look like? Why? What would you do differently if you looked like that person?
- What character in a book would you like to meet? Why?
- How do you deal with the stress of today?
- What century would you like to live in?
- What are the advantages and/or disadvantages of having a child?
- What would you do if you were the president?
- What is life like in the community in which you live?
- What is the most interesting place you've visited? Why?
- What was the most difficult thing you ever did?
- What can you tell your best friend?
- If you could change your house, what would it be like?
- What could make you very happy or very sad?
- What is an average day in your life like?
- If you could change anything about your life, what would it be?
- What would you like to be famous for and why?
- Do you think the average person has the ability to make a lot of money?
- How would your friends describe you?
- What is your favorite fairy tale? Why?
- What is your favorite cartoon? Why?
- What home projects do you like to do?
- What famous person from the past do you admire and why?
- How would you describe your children?
- What role do movie stars, athletes, and other celebrities play in society?
- How do you like to relax?
- Who is your favorite entertainer? Why?
- What will you do when you retire?
- What would you do today if you could do anything you wanted?
- Have you ever read a book that changed your life?
- What accomplishment are you proudest of?
- What is your favorite commerical? Why?
- What new skill have you learned recently? What was difficult about it and how did you learn it?

STORY ENDERS

- I have never been more frightened in my life.
- We had to buy it even though we really didn't want it anymore.
- That finally persuaded me to give up smoking.
- Then they gave me a bill for $500.
- That is a day I'd like to forget.
- It was a day I'll always remember.
- Now it has become a family joke.
- This event has changed my life forever.
- Now he/she is my personal hero/heroine.
- That's the last time I'll ever invite them over.
- It cost a lot of money, but it was worth it.
- It was the right choice.
- Obviously, I made the wrong choice.
- Then the lights went out.
- That's how he/she earned that nickname.
- Now my friends say I should be a race car driver.
- Everything he had said was a boldfaced lie.
- To this day, I won't eat that food.
- Now you can understand why I was so angry.
- That was the end of a miserable week.
- We'll never go back there again.
- I was tired but happy.
- That's when I realized I was an adult.
- It was the worst vacation we ever had.
- I finally decided to forgive and forget.

TIPS ON IMPROVING YOUR VOCABULARY

> Writers notice and collect words. Here are some tips that will help you make your vocabulary larger and more interesting.

1. Start a word bank. Whenever you come across a word that interests you, write it on a small word card made by cutting up 3" × 5" index cards. You might want to write the meaning of the word on the back of the card along with a sentence using the word. Put the cards in your word bank, which can be an envelope, a folder, or a small box.

2. Get familiar with a thesaurus. A **thesaurus** is a book that lists common words and their **synonyms**—words that mean the same or almost the same thing—and their **antonyms,** or opposites. Many of the synonyms will be new to you. As you learn about them, add them to your word bank.

3. Some nouns name certain groups of things. They are called **collective nouns.** Use them where they fit. Here are some examples:

colony of ants	gaggle of geese
crowd of people	herd of cattle
fleet of taxicabs	pride of lions
flock of sheep	swarm of mosquitos

    Do you know any others? Add whatever new collective nouns you find to your word bank.

4. Action verbs tell what the subject does. Look in your journal and list ten action verbs. Trade your list with a partner. Each can use the other's action verbs in sentences.

5. Some words echo the sounds they name, such as *buzz, crash, flop,* and *zoom.* Listen to the sounds around you. Make a list of other words that sound like the things they name. Add them to your word bank.

6. Trade an original story, description, or poem with a classmate. Find adjectives and adverbs your partner has used in his or her writing. Add the ones that interest you to your word bank.

7. Reread the last thing you wrote. List the verbs, nouns, pronouns, adverbs, adjectives, and conjunctions in separate columns. If you notice any interesting or unusual words, add them to your word bank.

LITERARY TERMS AND DEVICES

Here is a list of literary terms, including types of writing techniques, and elements of literature. Using some of these elements and devices correctly can add a new twist or bit of sparkle to your writing. The list may suggest something you've never used but might want to try out.

Alliteration. Alliteration occurs when two or more words have the same beginning consonant sound.

> Example: *Mike mixed some malt in his milk.*

Antonym. The antonym of a word is a word that has the opposite or nearly the opposite meaning. For example, *come-go* and *up-down* are antonyms. You can sometimes improve your writing by putting in an antonym for emphasis.

> Examples: *I mean* up, *not* down.
> *Tina didn't* ask *him to move, she* told *him to move.*

Here are a few antonyms:

large - small	**first - last**	**top - bottom**	**good - bad**
then - now	**old - young**	**clean - dirty**	**north - south**

Argument. An argument is a reason for holding a certain opinion. In persuasive writing, arguments are presented in order to convince readers to share the writer's opinion.

Cliché. A metaphor so frequently used that it has become an idiom or an expression with understood, but not literal, meaning

> Example: *Head of the class*

Cohesion. Cohesion refers to how well a story or article sticks together. This can be judged by seeing whether the parts relate to the whole and how much one part is referred to by another part. For example, a paragraph or sentence has cohesion if it refers to another paragraph or sentence used earlier in the work. Also see Ways of Organizing Your Thoughts (pages 116–118) and the entry in this section for Signal words .

Dialect. Dialect is a special way of speaking used by a particular group. A person's dialect may identify him or her as being from another time, place, or social group. Writers often try to duplicate the sound of a dialect, using alternate spellings and sentence structure.

> Example: *Ya'll come back now, ya heah?*

Dialogue. A dialogue refers to the words spoken by the characters in a story or play.

> Example: *Kevin asked, "What time will you be home tonight?"*
> *Marla answered, "Around 6:30."*

Note: Start a new paragraph each time you change speakers. Also note the use of quotation marks and commas to set off the words from their speaker.

Essay. An essay is a short composition that focuses on a single idea. It explains a writer's thoughts and opinions on one issue.

Fact. A fact is a statement that can be proven.

> Example: *In the United States there are about four million children at each grade level.*

Flashback. A break in the chronological sequence of a story in which an earlier incident is described.

Hyperbole. A hyperbole is an exaggeration.

> Example: *He must have been nine feet tall.*

Idiom. An expression that cannot be understood from the literal meaning of its words.

> Example: *Tom is barking up the wrong tree.*

Imagery. The author's use of description and words to create vivid pictures or images in the reader's mind.

> Example: *A blanket of soft snow covered the sleeping tractors.*

Irony. The use of tone, exaggeration, or understatement to suggest the opposite of the literal meaning of the words used. Irony can be related to sarcasm.

> Example: *I didn't mind waiting two hours; it was restful.*

Metaphor. A metaphor compares two things without using the words *like* or *as*.

> Example: *Habits are first cobwebs, then cables.*

Mood. The mood is a feeling the writer creates in the reader by including particular words, details, and images. Examples of different moods include peaceful, joyful, exciting, frightening, and angry.

Narrator. The narrator is the person who tells a story. The narrator may be a character in the story or may be an all-knowing person observing the action from outside the story. See also Point of view.

Onomatopoeia. Onomatopoeia is the term for words in which the sounds suggest the meaning of the words.

> Examples: *Ouch, bang, bow wow, ticktock, oink, crash.*

Opinion. An opinion is a statement of someone's belief or feelings. An opinion cannot be proven, but it can be based on facts.

> Example: *George is the best candidate.*

In a newspaper, editorials and letters from readers should contain opinions.

Personification. Giving a human quality or ability to an animal, object, or idea is called *personification.*

> Examples: *The wind whispered through the night.*
> *Friendly computers are easy to use.*

Point of view. Point of view refers to how an event or story looks to the narrator. In a story narrated from the first person point of view, the narrator is a character in the story and uses the first person pronouns *I, me, mine, we,* and *our.* In a story narrated from the third person point of view, the narrator is not part of the story and uses the third person pronouns *he, him, she, her,* or *them.*

Rhyme. Rhyme is the repetition of sounds at the ends of words. Some poems use rhyme in a repeating pattern.

> Example: *Twinkle, twinkle, little <u>star</u>,*
> *How I wonder what you <u>are</u>,*
> *Up above the world so <u>high</u>*
> *Like a diamond in the <u>sky</u>.*

Rhythm. Rhythm is the pattern of stressed and unstressed beats in poetry and prose.

Sensory details. Sensory details are words and phrases that appeal to the reader's five senses. They describe how a thing looks, sounds, smells, feels, or tastes.

> Example: *When I bit into the fuzzy peach, a sharp, sweet taste filled my mouth and sticky juice trickled down my chin.*

Signal words. Signal words tell the reader that there is a certain relationship between what has been stated already and what is coming up. Here are some specific kinds of signal words:

1. Continuation signals: *and, in addition, also*
2. Change of direction signals: *but, however, in contrast*
3. Sequence signals: *next, second, since, later*
4. Illustration signals: *for example, to illustrate, such as*
5. Emphasis signals: *remember that, the key feature, most important*
6. Cause, condition, or result signals: *if, while, due to, because*
7. Spatial signals: *under, between, on, close to*
8. Comparison-contrast signals: *less than, different from, same*
9. Conclusion signals: *in conclusion, in summary, therefore*
10. Uncertainty signals: *if, maybe, could, looks like, probably*
11. Nonword emphasis signals: exclamation point, underlined words, subheads in the text

Simile. A simile is a comparison of two things using the words *like* or *as*.

      Examples: *She felt as limp as a rag doll.*
                 The snow looked like a soft, white blanket.

(A metaphor also makes a comparison but without using the words *like* or *as*.)

Speaker. The speaker is the character the writer assumes. The speaker is not always the writer him- or herself. For example, in a poem written from the point of view of a dog, the dog is the speaker.

Symbol. A symbol is one thing that stands for another.

      Examples: *An owl stands for wisdom.*
                 A dove stands for peace.

Synonym. The synonym of a word is a word or phrase (short group of words) that has the same or about the same meaning. Be sure to use a synonym that means what you want to say. Here are a few examples of synonyms for *like*: *approve (of), appreciate, enjoy, love, adore.*

    A dictionary may have synonyms as part of each definition or in a separate list. A thesaurus lists both synonyms and antonyms.

Theme. The theme of a piece of writing is the single most important idea it is trying to communicate. The theme is sometimes called the *message* of the piece.

Tone. The tone of a piece of writing is its attitude. Examples of different tones include serious, humorous, reverent, sarcastic, and helpful.

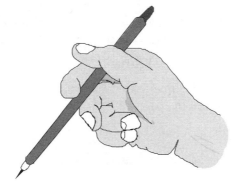

Teaching Suggestions_____

Teachers can help students get the most out of the *Writer's Manual* by explaining each section of it carefully and providing student activities based on it. Here are some suggested exercises to increase student proficiency in the skills they need to really benefit from this reference book.

The purpose of the following exercises is to familiarize students with the contents of the book so that they can easily locate the information they need to improve writing skills. Most of the exercises can be done in a class setting, with a small group, or one on one. You can use them to make up many more of your own sample questions, as well as entire lessons, presented in oral or written form. The first few exercises involving alphabetization require a great deal of practice, so giving students that practice, perhaps several times a week for several weeks, will teach them how the Spelling Checker can work for them.

Students should try to find the answers to the following exercise questions on their own, since an important goal of these activities is independence in learning to use the manual as a reference book. Students are not expected to know the answers, but they are expected to learn where to find the answers. If students ask how to spell a word during a writing exercise, for example, you can ask them to look it up in the book. When they turn in papers with spelling and punctuation errors, or friendly or business letters using incorrect form, refer them to the book for correct information.

Each section of the *Writer's Manual* provides the content for many lessons. For example, the section on punctuation suggests lessons on using the comma and apostrophe. The section on spelling rules suggests lessons on forming plurals or doubling the final letter when adding suffixes and word endings.

Finally, it will encourage students to know that even experienced writers have to look up the spelling of certain words or the rules for correct punctuation, and that all writers can benefit greatly from using reference works effectively.

Spelling Checker
Guide Letters
Pages 9–66

> Using just the letters at the top of the page, quickly find just the page on which each of the following words is located. Identify the page number.
>
> **wheel**   **obtain**   **February**
>
> (Note: For this exercise, don't take time to find the word; the purpose is to learn to use the guide letters at the top of the page.)

Spelling Checker
Alphabetization
Pages 9–66

> Find the following words, using first the guide letters at the top of the page, then the two-letter word group heading on the page. Identify the word listed just before each word below.
>
> **eagle**   **Sweden**   **polar**

Spelling Checker
Variant Forms
Pages 9–66

> What other word forms are in the word list for each of these root words?
>
> > **beg**　　　　**Spain**　　　　**vote**

Spelling Checker
Homophones
Pages 9–66

> For each of these words, supply another word that has the same sound but a different meaning.
>
> > **for**　　　　**weigh**　　　　**do**

Spelling Rules
Plurals and *S* Form of Verbs
Page 67

> How do you spell the plurals of *fox, candy,* and *knife*?

Spelling Rules
Adding Endings and Suffixes
Pages 67–68

> Add to each of these root words the suffix or ending listed.
>
> > **noise + y**　　　**marry + ed**　　　**hit + ing**
> > **rude + ly**　　　**cheerful + ly**　　**out + er**

Spelling Using Phonics
Pages 69–73

> What are three ways the long /a/ sound can be spelled?

Capitalization
Pages 74–75

> Name three groups of words that need to be written with a capital letter.

Punctuation
Pages 76–77

> Identify three situations in which you need to use a period.

The Apostrophe
Pages 78–79

> What are the three major uses of an apostrophe?

Abbreviations
Pages 80–82

What are the abbreviations for the following terms?

Maine	**A married woman**	**Monday**
Heights	**et cetera**	**adverb**

Grammar
Sentences
Pages 84–88

Add three modifiers (adjective, adverb, or prepositional phrase) to this sentence:

The player caught the ball.

Next, change the given sentence into a negative sentence.
Last, change it into a question.

Grammar
Verb Errors
Pages 89–92

Correct the following verb errors:
She sing very well.
She sing yesterday.
She sing tomorrow.
She sing in the shower now.

Grammar
Parts of Speech
Pages 93–94

What part of speech is each of the following words?

man	**run**	**beautiful**
beautifully	**and**	**they**

Types of Writing
Pages 95–96

Identify these classes of writing:
(1) three forms of writing; (2) three types of nonfiction; (3) three types of fiction.

The Writing Process
Pages 97–103

What are the five stages in the writing process?

Proofreading Symbols
Page 104

What is the symbol for starting a new paragraph?

Letter Forms
Pages 106–107

How does a business letter differ from a friendly letter?

Writing a Story and Writing About a Story
Pages 108–109

Describe the five stages of a typical plot.

Keeping a Daily Journal
Pages 110–111

Name three different things you might write about in your journal.

Writing a News Article
Page 113

Which two methods of ordering information should be used in organizing a news article?

Tips on Improving Your Vocabulary
Page 123

What are three ways to improve your vocabulary?

Literary Terms and Devices
Pages 124–127

Give your own example for each of the following terms:

alliteration	**onomatopoeia**	**antonym**
hyperbole	**idiom**	**metaphor**

Personal Spelling List
Pages 132–136

Name three kinds of words you should add to your personal spelling list.

Personal Spelling List _____

A lot of good writers keep a personal spelling list. Just writing a word in such a list will help you learn to spell the word, but the real time saver is that the next time you need to look up a word, you will find it much faster and more easily in a personal spelling list.

Your word list should include: (1) Words that you have had to look up in a dictionary. (2) Words that you often misspell. (3) Names of people, cities, and things not easily found in a dictionary or the Spelling Checker list. (4) Words unique to a subject such as biology, music, or sports. (5) Foreign words and phrases.

A _____   _____   _____

_____   _____   _____

_____   _____   _____

_____   _____   _____

B _____   _____   _____

_____   _____   _____

_____   _____   _____

_____   _____   _____

C _____   _____   _____

_____   _____   _____

_____   _____   _____

_____   _____   _____

D _____   _____   _____

_____   _____   _____

_____   _____   _____

_____   _____   _____

E

F

G

H

I

J _____ _____ _____

_____ _____ _____

_____ _____ _____

_____ _____ _____

_____ _____ _____

K _____ _____ _____

_____ _____ _____

_____ _____ _____

_____ _____ _____

L _____ _____ _____

_____ _____ _____

_____ _____ _____

_____ _____ _____

M _____ _____ _____

_____ _____ _____

_____ _____ _____

_____ _____ _____

N _____ _____ _____

_____ _____ _____

_____ _____ _____

O _____ _____ _____

_____ _____ _____

_____ _____ _____

P _____ _____ _____
_____ _____ _____
_____ _____ _____
_____ _____ _____

Q _____ _____ _____
_____ _____ _____
_____ _____ _____
_____ _____ _____

R _____ _____ _____
_____ _____ _____
_____ _____ _____
_____ _____ _____

S _____ _____ _____
_____ _____ _____
_____ _____ _____
_____ _____ _____

T _____ _____ _____
_____ _____ _____
_____ _____ _____
_____ _____ _____

U _____ _____ _____

_____ _____ _____

_____ _____ _____

_____ _____ _____

V _____ _____ _____

_____ _____ _____

_____ _____ _____

_____ _____ _____

W _____ _____ _____

_____ _____ _____

_____ _____ _____

_____ _____ _____

X _____ _____ _____

_____ _____ _____

Y _____ _____ _____

_____ _____ _____

_____ _____ _____

Z _____ _____ _____

_____ _____ _____

_____ _____ _____

INDEX

NOTES

NOTES

NOTES

NOTES

NOTES

NOTES